THE

BASEBALL

ULTIMATE
TRIVIA
BOOK

THE
BASEBALL
ULTIMATE
TRIVIA
BOOK

**Test Your Superfan Status
and Relive the Most Iconic
Baseball Moments**

Vincent Spada

EPIC INK

Contents

Introduction

Few sports conjure up a classic vision of America better than baseball. It is our national pastime, perhaps our earliest organized game, and has been with us through good times and bad. From its humble origins to its worldwide fascination, baseball captures what is best in the human character: effort, skill, determination, and, above all, teamwork and a desire to achieve something great.

But surprisingly—or perhaps unsurprisingly—the history of the game is a bit muddy. There is no definite time or date when the sport came into existence, as it was more or less cobbled together from many ballfields over the decades. The first reference to the word "base-ball" can be traced back to eighteenth-century England regarding a game called "rounders," which many consider to be the true origin of the modern sport. In North America, the first documented game took place in Canada in 1838—though some say Abner Doubleday "invented" baseball in Cooperstown, New York in 1839. However, Alexander Cartwright of New York City is generally considered to be the true inventor of what we now call Major League Baseball, forming the Knickerbocker Rules in 1845 and paving the way for the overall organization of the game.

Throughout the 1850s and 1860s, baseball grew in popularity and was even played by soldiers during the American Civil War on both sides. The first true professional team—the Cincinnati Red Stockings—formed in 1869, while the first true league, the National League, came together in 1876. The American League followed in 1901, with the champions of both leagues meeting in the first World Series in 1903.

The twentieth century began with the dead-ball era, which lasted until 1920, a period in which bats were heavier, baseballs were not wound as tight, and ballparks were large, all of which reduced batting averages and home runs. And then Babe Ruth appeared, the Sultan of Swat. A new game of homers took over and excited the fans, giving them hope during the troubles of the Great Depression. After World War II, Jackie Robinson made history by breaking the color barrier, and the game soon became a national obsession during the 1950s. Pitching took over in the 1960s and television made the sport accessible to all during the '70s and '80s, with the game only gaining in popularity in ensuing decades. Today, baseball has seen a resurgence of interest on a worldwide scale, with people from all over the world watching and playing, and new players and fans joining the ranks every day.

For this reason, we'd like to issue a friendly challenge to all those who love to think and talk baseball. So, grab a pal, put your thinking caps on, and let's get ready to play . . . **trivia!**

How to Use This Book

As of this writing, there are 30 Major League Baseball (MLB) teams. Each team is represented in the pages of this book. You will be tested with 20 questions for each squad, with the answers listed at the end of each chapter so you can see how you've performed. All questions in the book are current as of the end of the 2023 MLB season.

The questions for each team are divided into five sections of increasing difficulty. There are four questions per section, with point values assigned as follows:

- **Singles:** 1 point per question, 4 points maximum

- **Doubles:** 2 points per question, 8 points maximum

- **Triples:** 3 points per question, 12 points maximum

- **Home Runs:** 4 points per question, 16 points maximum

- **Playoffs/World Series:** The first question is worth 1 point, the second is worth 2 points, the third is worth 3 points, and the fourth is worth 4 points, for a maximum of 10 points available in this section

Where Do You RATE?

Here's a handy guide to how you measure up after you've answered all the questions and tallied your final score:

UP-AND-COMER
Point total of
300-599

Your baseball knowledge is well rounded, and you've definitely got some brain power. You've got a future in this game! Management has its eye on you.

ROOKIE
Point total of
299
or less

You answered some of the questions listed, at least—perhaps even hit a home run or two. Keep practicing. Before you know it, you'll be in the starting lineup!

ALL-STAR

Point total of

600–999

You clearly know your sport and would be a mainstay on any team! I have no doubt we'll be hearing about you for years to come.

HALL-OF-FAMER

Point total of

1,000

or higher

You are a baseball trivia legend! I bow to your extraordinary knowledge.

Scoring Sheet

AMERICAN LEAGUE

Baltimore Orioles __ / 50

Boston Red Sox __ / 50

Chicago White Sox __ / 50

Cleveland Guardians __ / 50

Detroit Tigers __ / 50

Houston Astros __ / 50

Kansas City Royals __ / 50

Los Angeles Angels __ / 50

Minnesota Twins __ / 50

New York Yankees __ / 50

Oakland Athletics __ / 50

Seattle Mariners __ / 50

Tampa Bay Rays __ / 50

Texas Rangers __ / 50

Toronto Blue Jays __ / 50

LEAGUE TOTAL: __ / 750

NATIONAL LEAGUE

Arizona Diamondbacks __ / 50

Atlanta Braves __ / 50

Chicago Cubs __ / 50

Cincinnati Reds __ / 50

Colorado Rockies __ / 50

Los Angeles Dodgers __ / 50

Miami Marlins __ / 50

Milwaukee Brewers __ / 50

New York Mets __ / 50

Philadelphia Phillies __ / 50

Pittsburgh Pirates __ / 50

San Diego Padres __ / 50

San Francisco Giants __ / 50

St. Louis Cardinals __ / 50

Washington Nationals __ / 50

LEAGUE TOTAL: __ / 750

GRAND TOTAL: __ / 1500

PLAY BALL!

Team Quizzes

AMERICAN League

Singles

1. What is the name of the famous street found just beyond right field at Oriole Park at Camden Yards?

A. Dawson Lane

B. Ripken Drive

C. Eutaw Street

D. Murray Way

2. In 2023, which Orioles fledgling took home AL Rookie of the Year honors?

A. Ryan Mountcastle

B. Adley Rutschman

C. Austin Hays

D. Gunnar Henderson

3. Which Baltimore pitcher was the Opening Day starter for the Birds in 2023?

A. Kyle Gibson

B. John Means

C. Kyle Bradish

D. Dean Kremer

4. Who is the winningest manger in Baltimore Orioles history, compiling a record of 1480–1060?

A. Cal Ripken Sr.

B. Earl Weaver

C. Buck Showalter

D. Joe Altobelli

Doubles

1. In what year did the St. Louis Browns move to Baltimore and become the Orioles?

A. 1965

B. 1958

C. 1955

D. 1954

2. Which player holds the Baltimore Orioles single-season team record for doubles, collecting 56 two-baggers in 2009?

A. Melvin Mora

B. Nick Markakis

C. Brian Roberts

D. Luke Scott

3. Which Baltimore icon took home the AL Rookie of the Year Award in 1982, as well as the AL MVP trophy in both 1983 and 1991?

A. Storm Davis

B. Don Baylor

C. Cal Ripken Jr.

D. Eddie Murray

4. Which player holds the Orioles single-season team record for home runs, launching 53 of them in 2013?

A. Chris Davis

B. Adam Jones

C. Matt Wieters

D. Brady Anderson

Triples

1. Which Baltimore pitcher won the AL Cy Young Award in 1969?

A. Pat Dobson

B. Mike Cuellar

C. Jim Palmer

D. Dave McNally

2. Which Orioles fielding phenom won 16 consecutive Gold Glove Awards from 1960–1975?

A. Larry Sheets

B. Boog Powell

C. Frank Robinson

D. Brooks Robinson

3. Name the Baltimore Orioles hero who took home AL Rookie of the Year honors in 1977.

A. Eddie Murray

B. Doug DeCinces

C. Rich Dauer

D. Gary Roenicke

4. Which Orioles all-timer captured the 1966 AL MVP Award while also winning the Triple Crown that season?

A. Boog Powell

B. Paul Blair

C. Frank Robinson

D. Don Buford

Home Runs

1. Which player holds the St. Louis Browns/Baltimore Orioles single-season team record for batting average with a mind-bending .420 clip and in what year did he register that mark?

A. George Sisler in 1922

B. Heinie Manush in 1928

C. George Sisler in 1920

D. Baby Doll Jacobson in 1921

2. Which player holds the Orioles single-season team record for most at-bats (AB) during a lone campaign with 673 AB?

A. Manny Machado

B. B. J. Surhoff

C. J. J. Hardy

D. Miguel Tejada

3. Which Orioles slugger led the AL in RBI in 1961, when he drove in 141 baserunners?

A. Boog Powell

B. Jim Gentile

C. Rocky Colavito

D. Whitey Herzog

4. Which hurler threw the first pitch in the modern history of the Baltimore Orioles in 1954?

A. Bob Turley

B. Joe Coleman

C. Lou Kretlow

D. Don Larsen

Playoffs / World Series

1. Which Orioles player was named MVP of the 1983 World Series against the Philadelphia Phillies, when the Birds captured their third world title?

A. Eddie Murray

B. John Shelby

C. Rick Dempsey

D. Jim Palmer

2. Name the Baltimore pitcher who spun a shutout in Game 2 of the 1966 World Series against the Los Angeles Dodgers and their opposing pitcher Sandy Koufax, appearing in his final game.

A. Jim Palmer

B. Moe Drabowsky

C. Wally Bunker

D. Scott McGregor

Baltimore iron man Cal Ripken Jr. played in a record 2,632 consecutive games from 1982–1998.

3. Orioles third baseman Brooks Robinson was named MVP of the 1970 World Series against the Cincinnati Reds. But what's the name of the other Orioles standout who also had nine hits in that series?

A. Davey Johnson

B. Mark Belanger

C. Bobby Grich

D. Paul Blair

4. Which boppin' Bird homered in Games 1 and 2 of the 1970 World Series, helping the Orioles win each by a single run?

A. Elrod Hendricks

B. Boog Powell

C. Merv Rettenmund

D. Don Buford

Answers: Singles: 1. C, 2. D, 3. A, 4. B; Doubles: 1. D, 2. C, 3. C, 4. A; Triples: 1. B, 2. D, 3. A, 4. C; Home Runs: 1. A, 2. B, 3. B, 4. D; Playoffs/World Series: 1. C, 2. A, 3. D, 4. B

BOSTON RED SOX

Singles

1. What is the name of the beloved Red Sox mascot who debuted in 1997?

A. Freddy the Fenway Friend

B. Roger the Red Sox Rocket

C. Timmy the Triple-Bagger

D. Wally the Green Monster

2. How high is the iconic left field wall in Fenway Park, known locally as "the Green Monster"?

A. 37 feet 4 inches

B. 38 feet 1 inch

C. 37 feet 2 inches

D. 37 feet 3 inches

3. What name did former Red Sox pitcher Mel Parnell give to the right field foul pole at Fenway Park?

A. Ted's Territory

B. Pesky's Pole

C. Rice's Wrap-Around

D. King Carl's Corner

4. The Boston Red Sox have retired 11 uniform numbers in their team history, but only one of them is of a former pitcher. Which legendary hurler wore number 45?

A. Pedro Martínez

B. Cy Young

C. Babe Ruth

D. Roger Clemens

Doubles

1. The AL club in Boston was renamed the Red Sox in 1908. What was the name they went by from 1901–1907?

A. Boston Pilgrims

B. Boston Puritans

C. Boston Americans

D. Boston Nationals

2. Which BoSox bat wizard won five AL batting titles in the 1980s, ending with a sparkling .328 career batting average?

A. Jim Rice

B. Mike Greenwell

C. Jody Reed

D. Wade Boggs

3. Which Red Sox legend led the AL with 22 home runs during the strike-shortened season of 1981?

A. Jim Rice

B. Carlton Fisk

C. Carl Yastrzemski

D. Dwight Evans

4. From which college did Boston draft Roger Clemens in the first round of the 1983 MLB June Amateur Draft?

A. Texas Christian University

B. University of Texas at Austin

C. Baylor University

D. Rice University

///

Triples

1. Which outfielder played with Boston from 1907–1915 and was known as "the Gray Eagle"?

A. Tris Speaker

B. Harry Hooper

C. Duffy Lewis

D. Tillie Walker

2. Which Boston rookie burst onto the scene in 1975, winning both the AL Rookie of the Year and MVP Awards?

A. Jim Rice

B. Tony Armas

C. Fred Lynn

D. Cecil Cooper

3. Which Red Sox player took home Rookie of the Year honors in 1972, also leading the AL in triples that season?

A. Carlton Fisk

B. Jerry Remy

C. Rick Burleson

D. Bernie Carbo

4. Which pitcher won 15 games for the Red Sox in 1978 despite only making three starts that season?

A. Dick Drago

B. Bob Stanley

C. Bill Lee

D. Jim Wright

Home Runs

1. How many career home runs did David Ortiz—"Big Papi"—hit while wearing a Red Sox uniform?

A. 477

B. 482

C. 498

D. 483

2. Which pitcher holds the Red Sox single-season team record for most saves at 46 and in what year did he gather that total?

A. Tom Gordon in 1999

B. Craig Kimbrel in 2018

C. Tom Gordon in 1998

D. Jonathan Papelbon in 2008

3. The 1967 Red Sox are known as the "Impossible Dream" team. Dick Williams was the manager, but who was the hitting coach on that unforgettable squad?

A. Bobby Doerr

B. Johnny Pesky

C. Ted Williams

D. Eddie Popowski

4. The Red Sox purchased the contract of nineteen-year-old Babe Ruth in 1914 for the alleged amount of $25,000. What team sold him to Boston?

A. Cleveland Spiders

B. Baltimore Terrapins

C. Philadelphia Athletics

D. Baltimore Orioles

Playoffs / World Series

1. Which Boston player socked a two-out, two-run homer in the top of the ninth in Game 5 of the 1986 American League Championship Series (ALCS) to give the Red Sox an improbable 6–5 lead over the California Angels?

A. Don Baylor

B. Dave Henderson

C. Jim Rice

D. Tony Armas

2. Which Red Sox player had homers in both Game 6 and Game 7 of the 2004 ALCS against the New York Yankees, helping Boston finally break the "Curse of the Bambino"?

A. Mark Bellhorn

B. Kevin Millar

C. Johnny Damon

D. Manny Ramirez

3. Carlton Fisk's walk-off home run for the BoSox in the 12th inning of Game 6 of the 1975 World Series is considered one of the most iconic moments in all of MLB history. Which Cincinnati Reds pitcher served it up?

A. Pedro Borbón

B. Pat Darcy

C. Rawly Eastwick

D. Will McEnaney

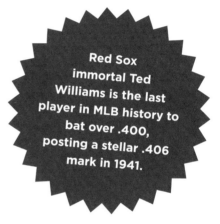

Red Sox immortal Ted Williams is the last player in MLB history to bat over .400, posting a stellar .406 mark in 1941.

4. Boston defeated the Pittsburgh Pirates 5–3 in the first-ever MLB World Series in 1903. Who was the winning pitcher for Boston in Game 8 of that historic contest?

A. Smoky Joe Wood

B. Tom Hughes

C. Bill Dinneen

D. Cy Young

Singles

1. Which White Sox player secured AL MVP honors in 2020, knocking in 60 runs during the 60-game season?

A. Yasmani Grandal

B. José Abreu

C. Tim Anderson

D. Paul Konerko

2. Name the ChiSox pitcher who earned 17 victories in 2012 and also fanned 192 batters.

A. Chris Sale

B. Jake Peavy

C. Gavin Floyd

D. Jose Quintana

3. Which former player/manager/owner had a ballpark named after him where the White Sox played from 1910–1990?

A. Connie Mack

B. Harry Frazee

C. Charles Comiskey

D. William Wrigley

4. Which Sox pitcher threw a no-hitter in 2007 against the Texas Rangers, followed by a perfect game against the Tampa Bay Rays in 2009?

A. Tom Seaver

B. Charlie Hough

C. Floyd Bannister

D. Mark Buehrle

Doubles

1. Name the White Sox icon who captured back-to-back AL MVP Awards in 1993 and 1994.

A. Frank Thomas

B. Bo Jackson

C. Robin Ventura

D. Ron Karkovice

2. Which Sox pitcher locked down 41 saves in 2006 and another 40 in 2007?

A. Dustin Hermanson

B. Dámaso Marte

C. Roberto Hernández

D. Bobby Jenks

3. Which Chicago ace won the AL Cy Young Award in 1993, posting 22 wins with four shutouts?

A. Alex Fernandez

B. Wilson Álvarez

C. Jack McDowell

D. Jason Bere

4. Which reliever holds the Chicago White Sox single-season team record for most saves with 57 and in what year did he notch this terrific total?

A. Roberto Hernández in 1991

B. Bobby Thigpen in 1990

C. Keith Foulke in 2001

D. Roberto Hernández in 1992

Triples

1. Which White Sox youngster nabbed the AL Rookie of the Year Award in 1983?

A. Greg Walker

B. Richard Dotson

C. Ron Kittle

D. Britt Burns

2. Also in 1983, which burly Chicago right-hander won the AL Cy Young Award?

A. Dennis Lamp

B. LaMarr Hoyt

C. Floyd Bannister

D. Jerry Reuss

3. The White Sox have retired number 3 in honor of which classy clutch character?

A. Billy Pierce

B. Ted Lyons

C. Harold Baines

D. Robin Ventura

4. Which Chicago White Sox player was named AL Rookie of the Year in 1985?

A. Ozzie Guillén

B. Scott Fletcher

C. Ray Durham

D. Daryl Boston

Home Runs

1. Which player holds the Chicago White Sox single-season team record for highest batting average, with an astounding .388 clip?

A. Joe Jackson
B. Eddie Collins
C. Luke Appling
D. Bibb Falk

2. Which White Sox great led the AL in hits four times and was named AL MVP in 1959?

A. Al Smith
B. Norm Cash
C. Ted Kluszewski
D. Nellie Fox

3. Name the ChiSox phenom who ran away with the AL Rookie of the Year Award in 1956 and led the AL in stolen bases for nine straight seasons from 1956–1964.

A. Billy Goodman
B. Luis Aparicio
C. Earl Torgeson
D. Sherm Lollar

4. Which Chicago White Sox hurler led the AL in wins in both 1925 and 1927?

A. Ted Lyons
B. Roy Wilkinson
C. Lefty Williams
D. Eddie Cicotte

The Chicago White Sox had the best record in the American League during their inaugural 1901 season, posting a pennant-winning mark of 83-53-1.

Playoffs / World Series

1. Which White Sox hero was crowned MVP of the 2005 World Series against the Houston Astros?

A. Geoff Blum

B. Paul Konerko

C. Aaron Rowand

D. Jermaine Dye

2. Which White Sox slugger walloped three homers and had 10 RBI in the 1959 World Series against the Los Angeles Dodgers?

A. Jim Landis

B. Ted Kluszewski

C. Jim Rivera

D. Frank Howard

3. Which Chicago pitcher tabbed three wins in the 1917 World Series, helping the White Sox defeat the New York Giants 4–2?

A. Red Faber

B. Eddie Cicotte

C. Dickey Kerr

D. Lefty Williams

4. The 1906 Chicago White Sox, known as the "Hitless Wonders," stunned the baseball world by winning their first-ever championship that season. Which team did they beat in the fall classic?

A. Boston Braves

B. Pittsburgh Pirates

C. Chicago Cubs

D. Brooklyn Dodgers

Answers: Singles: 1. B, 2. A, 3. C, 4. D; Doubles: 1. A, 2. D, 3. C, 4. B; Triples: 1. C, 2. B, 3. C, 4. A; Home Runs: 1. C, 2. D, 3. B, 4. A; Playoffs/World Series: 1. D, 2. B, 3. A, 4. C

CHICAGO WHITE SOX

37

CLEVELAND GUARDIANS

Singles

1. Which Cleveland clubber smacked 39 home runs and had 105 RBI in 2018, leading his squad to an AL Central title?

A. Francisco Lindor

B. Michael Brantley

C. José Ramírez

D. Edwin Encarnación

2. Cleveland has retired number 455. For whom and why was this done?

A. For the fans, in appreciation of 455 consecutive sellouts at home

B. For the owners, since a group of 455 individuals purchased the team

C. For the area code of the stadium's current location

D. For superstition, as that number is considered lucky in Ohio

3. Which Cleveland ace won AL Cy Young Awards in both 2014 and 2017?

A. Carlos Carrasco

B. Corey Kluber

C. Trevor Bauer

D. Josh Tomlin

4. Who is the all-time winningest manager in Cleveland history, racking up a record of 921–757?

A. Joe Gordon

B. Al López

C. Mike Hargrove

D. Terry Francona

Doubles

1. Which Cleveland speedster led the AL in stolen bases in five consecutive seasons from 1992–1996?

A. Carlos Baerga

B. Wayne Kirby

C. Mark Whiten

D. Kenny Lofton

2. Which Hall of Fame thumper swatted 612 home runs in his 22-year career, 337 of which were hit in a Cleveland uniform?

A. Albert Belle

B. Eddie Murray

C. Jim Thome

D. Manny Ramirez

3. Which Cleveland pitcher threw a perfect game against the Toronto Blue Jays on May 15, 1981—regarded as one of the greatest moments in Cleveland sports history?

A. Charles Nagy

B. John Denny

C. Bert Blyleven

D. Len Barker

4. Which Cleveland Hall of Fame ace led the AL in wins six times and won the pitching Triple Crown in 1940, and even started the season tossing a no-hitter on Opening Day?

A. Bob Feller

B. Early Wynn

C. Bob Lemon

D. Mike Garcia

Triples

1. Which heroic pioneer took the field with Cleveland in 1947, becoming the first-ever Black player in the American League?

A. Hank Aaron

B. Larry Doby

C. Willie Mays

D. Elston Howard

2. Which pitcher holds the Cleveland single-season team record for wins at 31 and in what year did he accomplish this milestone?

A. Addie Joss in 1907

B. George Uhle in 1926

C. Jim Bagby in 1920

D. Gaylord Perry in 1972

3. Which Cleveland hurler led the AL with 23 wins in 1954, helping his club capture an AL pennant that season?

A. Warren Spahn

B. Early Wynn

C. Hal Newhouser

D. Bob Lemon

4. Which player won AL MVP honors with Cleveland in 1948, batting .355 with 106 RBI?

A. Lou Boudreau

B. Joe Gordon

C. Ken Keltner

D. Dale Mitchell

Home Runs

1. Which Cleveland slugger won an AL MVP Award in 1953, belting 43 home runs with 145 RBI?

A. Jim Hegan

B. Al Rosen

C. Bobby Ávila

D. Wally Westlake

2. Which Cleveland outfielder had a year to end all years in 1936, leading the AL with 232 hits and 15 triples and posting a .378 batting average?

A. Joe Jackson

B. Hal Trosky

C. Earl Averill

D. Tris Speaker

3. Which Cleveland mound king won 20 or more games in four consecutive seasons from 1918–1921, earning 215 victories over his 14-year career?

A. Herb Score

B. Ray Caldwell

C. Smoky Joe Wood

D. Stan Coveleski

4. Which Cleveland standout had a fabulous campaign in 1904, leading the AL in hits (208), doubles (49), RBI (102), and batting average (.376)?

A. Joe Jackson

B. Tris Speaker

C. Charlie Hickman

D. Nap Lajoie

Playoffs / World Series

1. Which Cleveland player earned MVP honors for his terrific performance in the 2016 ALCS against the Toronto Blue Jays?

A. Andrew Miller

B. Francisco Lindor

C. Cody Allen

D. Bryan Shaw

2. Which Cleveland pitcher delivered seven shutout innings in Game 6 of the 1995 ALCS against the Seattle Mariners, guiding his squad to their first AL pennant in 41 years?

A. Ken Hill

B. Dennis Martínez

C. Charles Nagy

D. Orel Hershiser

3. Which Cleveland pitcher threw a complete game shutout against the Boston Braves in Game 3 of the 1948 World Series and also earned a save in Game 6 to end the whole show?

A. Gene Bearden

B. Russ Christopher

C. Herb Score

D. Satchel Paige

4. Cleveland won its first-ever World Series title in 1920 in memory of fallen teammate Ray Chapman. What team did they beat in the fall classic to memorialize their lost comrade?

A. Brooklyn Grooms

B. Brooklyn Superbas

C. Brooklyn Robins

D. Brooklyn Dodgers

Pitcher Bill Hart recorded the first win in Cleveland history, a complete game victory against the Chicago White Sox back in 1901.

Answers: Singles: 1. C, 2. A, 3. B, 4. D; Doubles: 1. D, 2. C, 3. D, 4. A; Triples: 1. B, 2. C, 3. B, 4. A; Home Runs: 1. B, 2. C, 3. D, 4. D; Playoffs/World Series: 1. A, 2. B, 3. A, 4. C

43

Singles

1. Which terrific Tigers player won the batting Triple Crown and AL MVP Award in 2012?

A. Prince Fielder
B. Delmon Young
C. Miguel Cabrera
D. Austin Jackson

2. Which Detroit ace won the pitching Triple Crown in 2011, as well as the AL Cy Young and MVP Awards that season?

A. Rick Porcello
B. Justin Verlander
C. Brad Penny
D. Max Scherzer

3. Which player cracked 33 home runs for the Tigers in 1984, leading Detroit to a World Series title?

A. Lance Parrish
B. Larry Herndon
C. Darrell Evans
D. Howard Johnson

4. Which Tigers staff ace led the team with 19 wins during that unforgettable 1984 campaign?

A. Juan Berenguer
B. Dan Petry
C. Milt Wilcox
D. Jack Morris

Doubles

1. Nicknamed "the Georgia Peach," which Tigers legend compiled more than 4,000 career hits?

A. Bobby Veach
B. Ty Cobb
C. Donie Bush
D. Al Kaline

2. Which Tigers pitcher baffled batters the entire season to take home both the AL Cy Young and MVP Awards in 1984?

A. Walt Terrell
B. Doyle Alexander
C. Willie Hernández
D. Frank Tanana

3. This Detroit youngster landed AL Rookie of the Year honors in 1978. Who was this classy cat?

A. Lou Whitaker

B. Kirk Gibson

C. Jason Thompson

D. Chet Lemon

4. Which Tigers player batted a lofty .343 in 1987, helping Detroit capture an AL East crown that season?

A. Matt Nokes

B. Bill Madlock

C. Alan Trammell

D. Tom Brookens

///

Triples

1. Which Hall of Famer holds the Detroit Tigers single-season team record for home runs with 58 and RBI with 184?

A. Rocky Colavito

B. Dale Alexander

C. Cecil Fielder

D. Hank Greenberg

2. Which Detroit-born Tigers pitching ace won 25 or more games three straight seasons from 1944–1946?

A. Dizzy Trout

B. Hal Newhouser

C. Virgil Trucks

D. Schoolboy Rowe

3. Detroit has retired number 23. Who wore these digits for the Tigers back in the day?

A. Willie Horton

B. Bill Freehan

C. Jim Northrup

D. Rudy York

4. Which iconic Tigers player recorded 3,007 career hits to go along with 399 home runs, all with Detroit?

A. Rocky Colavito

B. Harvey Kuenn

C. Walt Dropo

D. Al Kaline

Home Runs

1. Which Tigers player led the AL in hits and batting average in 1961, posting a staggering .361 clip?

A. Rocky Colavito

B. Ray Boone

C. Norm Cash

D. Bill Bruton

2. Which Detroit superstar led the AL in runs scored (131), hits (215), doubles (45), triples (19), and stolen bases (27) in 1929?

A. Charlie Gehringer

B. Harry Rice

C. Ty Cobb

D. Heinie Manush

3. Which Tigers legend holds the all-time MLB record for most career triples, with a total of 309?

A. Lu Blue

B. George Burns

C. Sam Crawford

D. Ty Cobb

4. Which Detroit Hall of Famer won four AL batting titles, including in 1923 with a .403 average?

A. Roy Johnson

B. Harry Heilmann

C. Bob Fothergill

D. Marty McManus

Playoffs / World Series

1. Which Tigers hero was the MVP of the 2012 ALCS against the New York Yankees?

A. Prince Fielder

B. Avisaíl García

C. Jhonny Peralta

D. Delmon Young

2. Which Detroit player smacked a walk-off home run in Game 4 of the 2006 ALCS against the Oakland A's to clinch the AL pennant for the Tigers?

A. Curtis Granderson

B. Magglio Ordóñez

C. Iván Rodríguez

D. Craig Monroe

3. In Game 5 of the 1984 fall classic against the San Diego Padres, which Tigers slugger hit an eighth inning home run to help ensure Detroit a world championship?

A. Kirk Gibson

B. Alan Trammell

C. Larry Herndon

D. Chet Lemon

4. Which Tigers pitcher bested St. Louis Cardinals ace Bob Gibson in Game 7 of the 1968 World Series, earning a complete game victory to clinch the title for Detroit?

A. Earl Wilson

B. Denny McLain

C. Mickey Lolich

D. Pat Dobson

Tigers ace Denny McLain notched 31 victories in 1968, making him the last MLB pitcher to win 30 or more games in a season.

Answers: Singles: 1. C, 2. B, 3. A, 4. D; Doubles: 1. B, 2. C, 3. A, 4. C; Triples: 1. D, 2. B, 3. A, 4. D; Home Runs: 1. C, 2. A, 3. C, 4. B; Playoffs/World Series: 1. D, 2. B, 3. A, 4. C

HOUSTON ASTROS

Singles

1. Which player did the Astros select with their *second* first-round pick in the 2015 MLB June Amateur Draft?

A. Kyle Tucker

B. Carlos Correa

C. George Springer

D. Alex Bregman

2. Which Astros slugger burst onto the scene in 2019, winning the AL Rookie of the Year award?

A. Myles Straw

B. Teoscar Hernández

C. Yordan Alvarez

D. Colby Rasmus

3. Which Astros player led the AL in hits four consecutive seasons, from 2014–2017?

A. Jose Altuve

B. Carlos Correa

C. George Springer

D. Josh Reddick

4. Which Astros slugger led the AL with 51 doubles in 2018?

A. Evan Gattis

B. Yuli Gurriel

C. Carlos Beltrán

D. Alex Bregman

Doubles

1. In what year did the Houston franchise debut and play its first MLB game?

A. 1961

B. 1962

C. 1966

D. 1963

2. Under which name did the Houston team play during its first three seasons?

A. Wranglers

B. Alamos

C. Colt .45s

D. Gunslingers

3. How many hits did Astros legend Craig Biggio tally during his 20-year career?

A. 2,998

B. 3,060

C. 3,074

D. 3,123

4. Which Houston player took home the NL Rookie of the Year Award in 1991 and NL MVP honors in 1994?

A. Ken Caminiti

B. Luis González

C. Steve Finley

D. Jeff Bagwell

Triples

1. Which Astros ace earned the NL Cy Young Award for his standout performance in 1986?

A. Nolan Ryan

B. Bob Knepper

C. Mike Scott

D. Jim Deshaies

2. Closer Billy Wagner had 422 career saves. How many of them came in an Astros uniform?

A. 201

B. 225

C. 255

D. 270

3. Which Houston player smashed 31 homers and had 101 RBI in 1986, helping the Astros clinch the NL West?

A. José Cruz

B. Terry Puhl

C. Kevin Bass

D. Glenn Davis

4. Which Astros hurler led the team with 20 victories during the 1976 campaign?

A. J. R. Richard

B. Larry Dierker

C. Nolan Ryan

D. Joaquín Andújar

Home Runs

1. Which player collected the first hit in Houston franchise history?

A. Román Mejías

B. Joe Morgan

C. Bob Aspromonte

D. Hal Smith

2. Which thumper holds the Houston Astros single-season team RBI record with 136?

A. Moisés Alou

B. Lance Berkman

C. Roger Metzger

D. Richard Hidalgo

3. Which powerhouse Houston player was known as "the Toy Cannon"?

A. Jimmy Wynn

B. Rusty Staub

C. Enos Cabell

D. Joe Morgan

4. Which pitcher holds the Houston Astros single-season team win record with 22 victories?

A. Roy Oswalt

B. José Lima

C. Joe Niekro

D. Mike Hampton

Former Astros Hall of Fame ace Nolan Ryan holds the all-time MLB record for career strikeouts with 5,714 batters whiffed. Ryan also holds the MLB record for career no-hitters, tossing seven of them in his amazing 27 seasons in the big leagues.

Playoffs / World Series

1. Which Astros player earned MVP honors for his fine performance in the 2022 World Series against the Philadelphia Phillies?

A. Cristian Javier

B. Jeremy Peña

C. Chas McCormick

D. Framber Valdez

2. Which Astros hurler earned the victory in Game 7 of the 2017 World Series against the Los Angeles Dodgers, securing Houston's first-ever world championship?

A. Brad Peacock

B. Francisco Liriano

C. Charlie Morton

D. Chris Devenski

3. Which Houston player was named MVP of the 2005 NLCS against the St. Louis Cardinals, helping the Astros win their first-ever NL pennant?

A. Morgan Ensberg

B. Chris Burke

C. Brad Lidge

D. Roy Oswalt

4. Which Houston batter homered off New York Mets pitcher Jesse Orosco in the 14th inning of Game 6 in that wild and memorable 1986 NLCS?

A. Billy Hatcher

B. Denny Walling

C. Alan Ashby

D. Craig Reynolds

Answers: Singles: 1. A, 2. C, 3. A, 4. D; Doubles: 1. B, 2. C, 3. B, 4. D; Triples: 1. C, 2. B, 3. D, 4. A; Home Runs: 1. C, 2. B, 3. A, 4. D; Playoffs/World Series: 1. B, 2. C, 3. D, 4. A

Kansas City *Royals*

Singles

1. Which Royals all-star led the AL with 48 homers and 121 RBI in 2021?

A. Vinnie Pasquantino

B. Carlos Santana

C. Hunter Dozier

D. Salvador Perez

2. Which Kansas City rookie cracked 20 homers and had 80 RBI in his 2022 freshman campaign?

A. Jorge Soler

B. Bobby Witt Jr.

C. Ryan O'Hearn

D. Michael Massey

3. Which Royals player led the AL with 51 doubles in 2012?

A. Eric Hosmer

B. Billy Butler

C. Alex Gordon

D. Mike Moustakas

4. Which Kansas City ace captured the AL Cy Young Award in 2009?

A. Zack Greinke

B. Luke Hochevar

C. Danny Duffy

D. Gil Meche

Doubles

1. Which Royals future Hall of Famer batted a phenomenal .390 in 1980, earning AL MVP honors?

A. Amos Otis

B. Willie Aikens

C. Al Cowens

D. George Brett

2. Which Kansas City pitcher earned AL Cy Young Awards in both 1985 and 1989?

A. Danny Jackson

B. Bud Black

C. Bret Saberhagen

D. Mark Gubicza

3. Which Royals second baseman captured six consecutive AL Gold Glove Awards from 1977–1982?

A. Kevin Seitzer

B. Buddy Biancalana

C. Kurt Stillwell

D. Frank White

4. In 1989, which sports phenom led the Royals with 32 homers and 105 RBI?

A. Danny Tartabull

B. Bo Jackson

C. Deion Sanders

D. Brian McRae

Triples

1. Which Royals speedster led the AL in triples five times—1980, 1982, 1985, 1987, and 1988?

A. Willie Wilson

B. Johnny Damon

C. Lonnie Smith

D. Rudy Law

2. Which Kansas City reliever led the AL in saves four consecutive seasons from 1982–1985?

A. Gene Garber

B. Jeff Montgomery

C. Dan Quisenberry

D. Steve Farr

3. Which Royals player led the AL with 133 RBI in 1982?

A. Hal McRae

B. Jorge Orta

C. Darryl Motley

D. Steve Balboni

4. Which Kansas City pitcher won 18 games in 1993, also capturing the AL earned run average (ERA) title that season?

A. Mark Gubicza

B. Kevin Appier

C. Tom Gordon

D. David Cone

Home Runs

1. Which pitcher holds the Royals single-season team record for strikeouts with 244?

A. James Shields

B. Bob Johnson

C. Danny Duffy

D. Dennis Leonard

2. Which Kansas City player led the AL with 53 stolen bases in 1977?

A. U. L. Washington

B. John Wathan

C. Freddie Patek

D. Al Cowens

3. In 1973, who became the first Kansas City Royals pitcher to win at least 20 games in a season?

A. Dick Drago

B. Paul Splittorff

C. Larry Gura

D. Jim Colborn

4. Which Royals all-star led the AL with 207 hits in 1987?

A. Kevin Seitzer

B. Ángel Salazar

C. Gerald Perry

D. Gregg Jefferies

Former Royals pitching ace Steve Busby threw the first no-hitter in Kansas City Royals history—the first of two no-hitters he would toss in his short but brilliant career.

Playoffs / World Series

1. Which Royals player grabbed MVP honors for his clutch hitting in the 2014 ALCS against the Baltimore Orioles?

A. Omar Infante

B. Lorenzo Cain

C. Alcides Escobar

D. Mike Moustakas

2. In Game 1 of the 2015 World Series, whose walk-off sacrifice fly in the 14th inning brought home the winning run for the Royals?

A. Ben Zobrist

B. Alex Ríos

C. Kendrys Morales

D. Eric Hosmer

3. In the ninth inning of Game 6 of the 1985 World Series, what was the name of the first base umpire who made the infamous "safe" call in favor of the Royals?

A. Jim Quick

B. Jim McKean

C. Don Denkinger

D. Richard Shulock

4. In Game 6 of the 1985 World Series, which Royals batter delivered a clutch two-run single in the ninth inning to clinch the contest for Kansas City?

A. Dane Iorg

B. Pat Sheridan

C. Jim Sundberg

D. Garth Iorg

Answers: Singles: 1. D, 2. B, 3. C, 4. A; Doubles: 1. D, 2. C, 3. D, 4. B; Triples: 1. A, 2. C, 3. A, 4. B; Home Runs: 1. D, 2. C, 3. B, 4. A; Playoffs/World Series: 1. B, 2. D, 3. C, 4. A

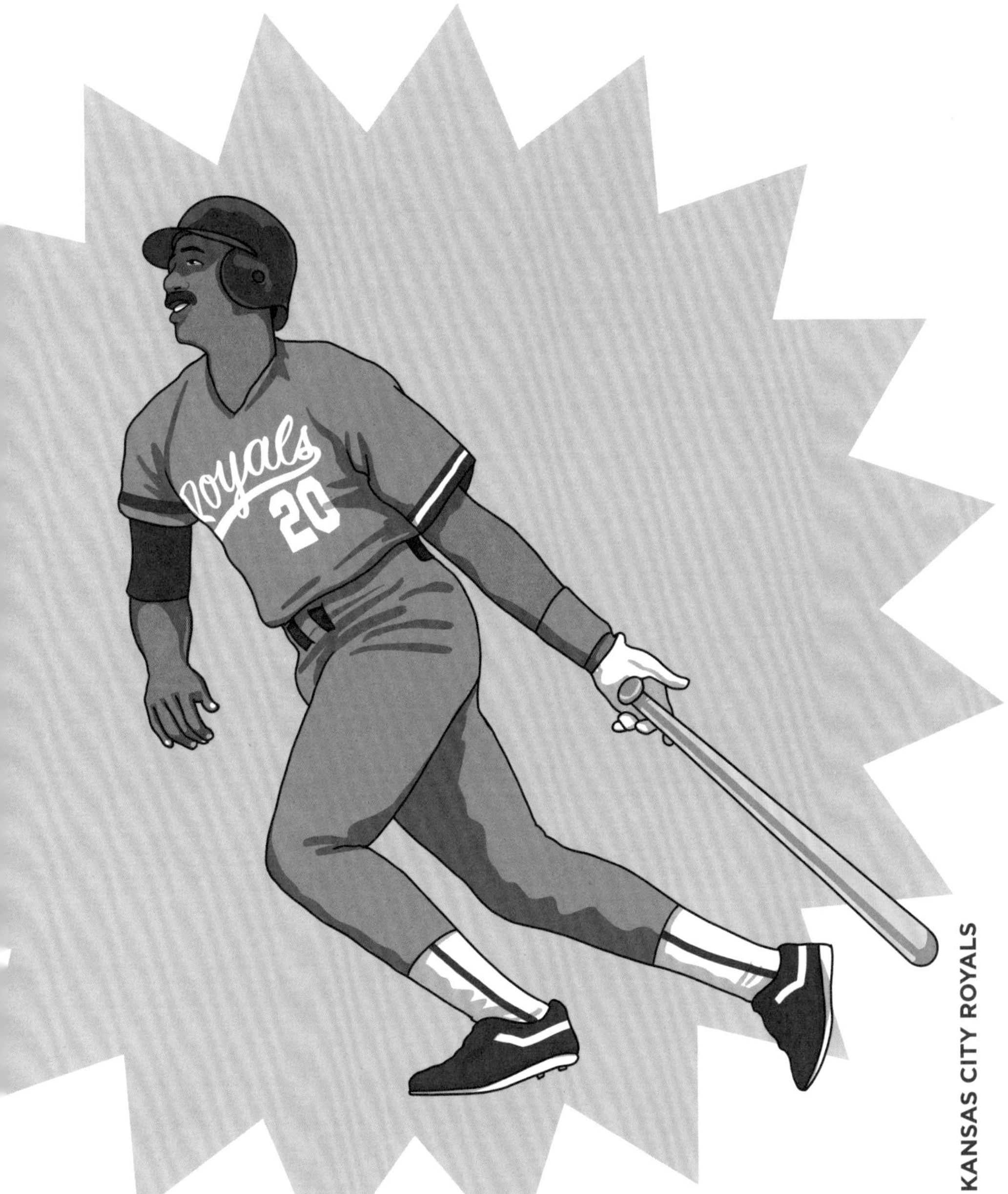
Royals
20

LOS ANGELES ANGELS

Singles

1. Which Angels superstar won AL Rookie of the Year honors in 2012 and three AL MVP Awards in 2014, 2016, and 2019?

A. Vernon Wells

B. Mike Trout

C. Torii Hunter

D. Peter Bourjos

2. Which Angels phenom captured the AL Rookie of the Year Award in 2018 and won two AL MVP trophies in 2021 and 2023?

A. Justin Upton

B. Taylor Ward

C. Jared Walsh

D. Shohei Ohtani

3. Which Anaheim Angels player took home the AL MVP Award in 2004?

A. Vladimir Guerrero

B. Troy Glaus

C. José Guillén

D. Adam Kennedy

4. Which Los Angeles Angels shortstop won consecutive Gold Glove Awards in 2017–2018?

A. David Fletcher

B. Jose Iglesias

C. Andrelton Simmons

D. David Eckstein

Doubles

1. Which Angels great took home the AL Rookie of the Year Award in 1993?

A. J. T. Snow

B. Damion Easley

C. Jim Edmonds

D. Tim Salmon

2. Which Angels pitcher tossed a no-hitter against the Minnesota Twins on May 2, 2012?

A. Ervin Santana

B. Jered Weaver

C. Jeff Weaver

D. Kelvim Escobar

3. Which player holds the Los Angeles Angels single-season team record for both hits (240) and batting average (.355)—a feat he accomplished in the same year?

A. Rod Carew

B. Darin Erstad

C. Chone Figgins

D. Alex Johnson

4. Name the Angels reliever who set the MLB single-season record for saves with a staggering 62 game-ending lockdowns in 2008.

A. Francisco Rodríguez

B. Huston Street

C. Troy Percival

D. Bryan Harvey

Triples

1. Which Anaheim Angels slugger led the AL with 47 home runs in 2000?

A. Jim Edmonds

B. Garret Anderson

C. Troy Glaus

D. Mo Vaughn

2. Which California Angels hurler led the staff with 18 wins in 1990?

A. Mark Langston

B. Jim Abbott

C. Kirk McCaskill

D. Chuck Finley

3. Which Angels rookie smacked 22 homers and had 100 RBI in 1986, helping California capture an AL West title?

A. Dick Schofield

B. Devon White

C. Wally Joyner

D. Brian Downing

4. Which California Angels ace pitched a perfect game against the Texas Rangers on the final day of the 1984 season?

A. Mike Witt

B. Don Sutton

C. Tommy John

D. John Candelaria

Home Runs

1. Which Angels slugger led the AL with 139 RBI in 1979, helping him earn AL MVP honors?

A. Carney Lansford

B. Don Baylor

C. Doug DeCinces

D. Brian Downing

2. During the 1981 strike-shortened season, which California Angels player led the AL with 22 home runs?

A. Fred Lynn

B. Dan Ford

C. Butch Hobson

D. Bobby Grich

3. Which Angels hurler led the AL with 269 strikeouts in 1975?

A. Frank Tanana

B. Nolan Ryan

C. Ed Figueroa

D. Bill Singer

4. Which fleet-footed California Angels player led the AL with 13 triples in 1968?

A. Don Mincher

B. Buck Rodgers

C. Jim Fregosi

D. Roger Repoz

Playoffs / World Series

1. In Game 5 of the 2002 ALCS against the Minnesota Twins, which Angels player cranked three home runs, winning series MVP and lifting his squad to their first-ever AL pennant?

A. Adam Kennedy

B. Brad Fullmer

C. Garret Anderson

D. Bengie Molina

2. Despite losing the 1986 ALCS to the Red Sox, which California Angels player gave a great effort by collecting 10 hits to go along with a .455 batting average?

A. Rob Wilfong

B. Bob Boone

C. Reggie Jackson

D. Gary Pettis

3. Down 5–0 to the San Francisco Giants in Game 6 of the 2002 World Series, which Angels player hit a clutch seventh-inning home run, helping Anaheim rally to an improbable 6–5 win?

A. Garret Anderson

B. Chone Figgins

C. Alex Ochoa

D. Scott Spiezio

4. In Game 7 of the 2002 World Series, name the hurler who picked up the win to secure the Angels' first-ever title flag.

A. Brendan Donnelly

B. Troy Percival

C. John Lackey

D. Jarrod Washburn

The Angels were once owned by Gene Autry, "the Singing Cowboy," whose hit songs included "Here Comes Santa Claus" and "Rudolph, the Red-Nosed Reindeer."

Answers: Singles: 1. B, 2. D, 3. A, 4. C; Doubles: 1. D, 2. B, 3. B, 4. A; Triples: 1. C, 2. D, 3. C, 4. A; Home Runs: 1. B, 2. D, 3. A, 4. C; Playoffs/World Series: 1. A, 2. B, 3. D, 4. C

MINNESOTA *Twins*

Singles

1. Which talented Twins player led his squad with 28 homers in 2022?

A. Carlos Correa

B. José Miranda

C. Max Kepler

D. Byron Buxton

2. Which Minnesota Hall of Famer took home the AL MVP Award in 2009?

A. Michael Cuddyer

B. Jason Kubel

C. Denard Span

D. Joe Mauer

3. Name the Twins ace who captured AL Cy Young Awards in both 2004 and 2006, winning the pitching Triple Crown in the latter season.

A. Kyle Lohse

B. Johan Santana

C. Brad Radke

D. Carlos Silva

4. Which Minnesota thumper slugged his way to an AL MVP Award in 2006?

A. Nelson Cruz

B. Rondell White

C. Justin Morneau

D. Torii Hunter

Doubles

1. In what year did the Washington Senators move to Minnesota and become the Twins?

A. 1961

B. 1962

C. 1965

D. 1964

2. Which Minnesota Twins all-timer led the AL in hits four times (1987–1989 and 1992)?

A. Tom Brunansky

B. Kirby Puckett

C. Gary Gaetti

D. Greg Gagne

3. Which terrific Twins player finished second in AL Rookie of the Year voting in 1982, batting .301 with 23 homers and 92 RBI?

A. Tim Laudner

B. Randy Bush

C. Kent Hrbek

D. Steve Lombardozzi

4. Which Minnesota player gloved the AL Rookie of the Year award in 1991?

A. Chuck Knoblauch

B. Paul Sorrento

C. Scott Leius

D. Al Newman

//

Triples

1. Which Twins pitcher tallied 24 wins in 1970, earning himself an AL Cy Young Award that season?

A. Luis Tiant

B. Jim Perry

C. Bert Blyleven

D. Jim Kaat

2. Name the Hall of Fame Minnesota hitting machine who batted his way to an AL Rookie of the Year Award in 1964.

A. Earl Battey

B. Bob Allison

C. Tony Oliva

D. Jimmie Hall

3. Which Twins player led the AL in runs scored, doubles, and triples in 1965, and won an MVP Award that season?

A. Harmon Killebrew

B. Rich Rollins

C. Zoilo Versalles

D. Vic Power

4. Which marvelous Minnesota all-star won the AL Rookie of the Year Award in 1967 and the AL MVP Award in 1977, a season in which he batted an astounding .388?

A. Lyman Bostock

B. Harmon Killebrew

C. Larry Hisle

D. Rod Carew

//

Home Runs

1. How many career home runs did Twins Hall of Fame legend Harmon Killebrew hit in his 22 big-league seasons?

A. 573

B. 577

C. 579

D. 580

2. Before moving to Minnesota, the Twins were the Washington Senators/Nationals, and the team's all-time pitcher Walter Johnson holds the MLB record for most career shutouts. How many did he record during his glorious 21-year career?

A. 107

B. 115

C. 122

D. 110

3. Which Senators/Nationals Hall of Famer led the AL in hits in both 1924 and 1926?

A. Bucky Harris

B. Sam Rice

C. Nemo Leibold

D. Joe Judge

4. Which Senators/Nationals Hall of Famer led the AL with a .379 BA in 1928?

A. Goose Goslin

B. Red Barnes

C. Joe Cronin

D. George Sisler

Playoffs / World Series

1. In Game 7 of the 1991 World Series, which Twins all-time hero delivered the walk-off hit in the 10th inning to win the whole show?

A. Mike Pagliarulo

B. Brian Harper

C. Gene Larkin

D. Chili Davis

2. In Game 6 of the 1991 World Series, Minnesota superstar Kirby Puckett cracked a walk-off home run in the 11th inning to even things up at 3–3. Which Atlanta Braves pitcher had the misfortune of serving up that Homer Hanky home run?

A. Charlie Leibrandt

B. Mike Stanton

C. Steve Avery

D. Alejandro Peña

3. Which Twins player smacked a grand slam in Game 1 of the 1987 World Series, leading his team to a 10–1 victory?

A. Steve Lombardozzi

B. Tom Brunansky

C. Greg Gagne

D. Dan Gladden

4. In Game 7 of the 1924 World Series, which Senators/Nationals player delivered a walk-off hit in the 12th inning to capture the first-ever title flag for the city of Washington, D.C.?

A. Curly Ogden

B. Earl McNeely

C. Muddy Ruel

D. Ossie Bluege

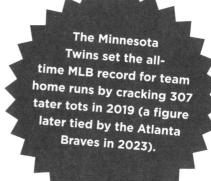

The Minnesota Twins set the all-time MLB record for team home runs by cracking 307 tater tots in 2019 (a figure later tied by the Atlanta Braves in 2023).

NEW YORK YANKEES

Singles

1. Which talented Yankees rookie infielder took home a Gold Glove Award in 2023?

A. Gleyber Torres

B. Anthony Volpe

C. Oswaldo Cabrera

D. Oswald Peraza

2. Which Yankees fireballer blazed his way to an AL Cy Young Award in 2023?

A. Gerrit Cole

B. Nestor Cortes

C. Clarke Schmidt

D. Carlos Rodón

3. Name the Bronx Bomber who won the AL Rookie of the Year Award in 2017 and AL MVP trophy in 2022, setting an AL record with 62 home runs that season.

A. Anthony Rizzo

B. Joey Gallo

C. Aaron Judge

D. Giancarlo Stanton

4. Which Yankees player hit his way to an AL batting title in 2020?

A. Brett Gardner

B. Luke Voit

C. Gio Urshela

D. DJ LeMahieu

Doubles

1. Which speedster holds the Yankees' single-season team record for stolen bases with 93 bags swiped in 1988?

A. Snuffy Stirnweiss

B. Wille Randolph

C. Rickey Henderson

D. Dave Winfield

2. Which Yankees all-timer won an AL batting title in 1984 and an AL MVP Award in 1985?

A. Dave Winfield

B. Don Mattingly

C. Don Baylor

D. Mike Pagliarulo

3. Which team surrendered Yankees Hall of Fame shortstop Derek Jeter's first MLB hit in 1995?

A. Boston Red Sox

B. Chicago White Sox

C. Seattle Mariners

D. Baltimore Orioles

4. How many career saves did legendary Yankees reliever Mariano Rivera record during his 19 seasons in the Bronx?

A. 652

B. 653

C. 655

D. 662

3. Which two Cleveland pitchers stopped Joe DiMaggio's incredible 56-game hitting streak in 1941?

A. Al Milnar and Clint Brown

B. Al Smith and Jim Bagby Jr.

C. Bob Feller and Steve Gromek

D. Bob Feller and Joe Heving

///

Triples

1. Which Yankees immortal won the AL Rookie of the Year Award in 1970 and the AL MVP trophy in 1976?

A. Roy White

B. Reggie Jackson

C. Graig Nettles

D. Thurman Munson

4. How many career home runs did Yankees Hall of Famer Mickey Mantle hit during his 18 unforgettable big-league seasons?

A. 534

B. 536

C. 537

D. 538

2. Name the Yankees ace who won 25 games in 1961, earning him the AL Cy Young Award that season.

A. Whitey Ford

B. Bob Turley

C. Ralph Terry

D. Red Ruffing

Home Runs

1. Which Yankees great earned AL MVP honors in both 1960 and 1961?

A. Yogi Berra

B. Tony Kubek

C. Roger Maris

D. Johnny Mize

2. Under what name did the Yankees play from 1903–1912?

A. The New York Grandstanders

B. The New York Lowlanders

C. The New York Midlanders

D. The New York Highlanders

3. How many consecutive games did iconic Yankees first baseman Lou Gehrig, "the Iron Horse," play in before his streak ended on May 2, 1939?

A. 2,130

B. 2,132

C. 2,134

D. 2,140

4. Babe Ruth holds the Yankees' single-season team record for batting average. What was that average and in what year did he accomplish this marvelous feat?

A. .378 in 1921

B. .393 in 1923

C. .376 in 1920

D. .373 in 1927

Playoffs / World Series

1. Which Yankees fan-favorite was named MVP of the 2009 World Series against the Philadelphia Phillies?

A. Hideki Matsui

B. Derek Jeter

C. Mariano Rivera

D. Alex Rodriguez

2. How many games total, both regular season and playoffs, did the Yankees win during their spectacular championship year of 1998?

A. 122

B. 123

C. 124

D. 125

3. Reggie Jackson cracked three home runs in Game 6 of the 1977 World Series. Name the three Dodgers pitchers who surrendered those famous gopher balls.

A. Burt Hooton, Elías Sosa, Bob Welch

B. Don Sutton, Tommy John, Bob Welch

C. Tommy John, Elías Sosa, Charlie Hough

D. Burt Hooton, Elías Sosa, Charlie Hough

4. In what year did the Yankees win their first-ever World Series title, who did they beat in the fall classic, and who was the Yanks' manager that season?

A. 1921, Chicago Cubs, Bob Shawkey

B. 1922, Boston Braves, Clark Griffith

C. 1923, New York Giants, Miller Huggins

D. 1927, Pittsburgh Pirates, Joe McCarthy

The Yankees retired number 8 twice in honor of two of their all-time great players, both catchers: Bill Dickey and Yogi Berra.

OAKLAND ATHLETICS

Singles

1. Which Athletics slugger led the AL with 48 home runs in 2018?

A. Matt Olson

B. Matt Chapman

C. Mark Canha

D. Khris Davis

2. Which three players won AL Rookie of the Year Awards for the Athletics during the 2000s?

A. Tim Hudson, Mark Mulder, Barry Zito

B. Jason Giambi, Eric Chavez, Terrence Long

C. Ramón Hernández, Mark Ellis, Eric Byrnes

D. Bobby Crosby, Huston Street, Andrew Bailey

3. Name the Oakland bopper who took home the AL MVP Award in 2002.

A. Jason Giambi

B. Scott Hatteberg

C. Miguel Tejada

D. Eric Chavez

4. Which Athletics player earned an AL Rookie of the Year Award in 1998?

A. Ben Grieve

B. A.J. Hinch

C. Ryan Christenson

D. José Herrera

Doubles

1. Which Oakland A's ace played it cool on his way to winning the AL Cy Young Award in 2002?

A. Mark Mulder

B. Barry Zito

C. Tim Hudson

D. Aaron Harang

2. How many stolen bases did A's superstar Rickey Henderson record during his electric 25-year career?

A. 1,366

B. 1,404

C. 1,406

D. 1,458

3. How many home runs did Oakland's Mark McGwire hit during his baseball-bashing AL Rookie of the Year season in 1987?

A. 48

B. 49

C. 50

D. 51

4. Which Athletics bomber captured the AL Rookie of the Year Award in 1986 and AL MVP honors in 1988?

A. Dave Henderson

B. Dave Parker

C. Don Baylor

D. Jose Canseco

Oakland slugger Tony Armas led the AL with 22 home runs during the strike-shortened season of 1981.

Triples

1. A's MVP Reggie Jackson, known as "Mr. October," hit 563 regular season home runs during his 21-year career. How many longshots did he hit in his 77 career playoff games?

A. 18

B. 23

C. 24

D. 25

2. Which Athletics pitcher tossed a perfect game against the Minnesota Twins in 1968 and won the AL Cy Young Award in 1974?

A. Blue Moon Odom

B. Vida Blue

C. Catfish Hunter

D. Ken Holtzman

3. How many times did Oakland's great reliever Rollie Fingers lead the AL in saves while pitching for the Athletics?

A. 0

B. 3

C. 4

D. 6

4. Name the magnificent Oakland A's hurler who won both the AL Cy Young and MVP Awards in 1971.

A. Blue Moon Odom

B. Vida Blue

C. Chuck Dobson

D. Ken Holtzman

Home Runs

1. Which Athletics two-time AL MVP slugged 58 home runs in 1932 and 48 more dingers in 1933?

A. Jimmy Dykes

B. Mule Haas

C. Max Bishop

D. Jimmie Foxx

2. Which Athletics all-timer took home the AL MVP title in 1928?

A. Mickey Cochrane

B. Tris Speaker

C. Ty Cobb

D. Max Bishop

3. Which legendary A's pitcher captured the AL MVP Award in 1931 by winning an astounding 31 games?

A. Rube Waddell

B. Charles Bender

C. Lefty Grove

D. Eddie Plank

4. Name the player who holds the Athletics' single-season team record for batting average with an eye-popping .426 mark.

A. Eddie Collins

B. Al Simmons

C. Nap Lajoie

D. Ty Cobb

///

Playoffs / World Series

1. Which Oakland ace spun a complete game shutout in Game 1 of the 1989 World Series?

A. Mike Moore

B. Dave Stewart

C. Storm Davis

D. Bob Welch

2. Which A's player belted four home runs against the Reds on his way to being named MVP of the 1972 fall classic?

A. George Hendrick

B. Gene Tenace

C. Joe Rudi

D. Reggie Jackson

3. Name the Athletics player who delivered a clutch game-winning single in the 11th inning of Game 3 of the 1973 World Series.

A. Bert Campaneris

B. Sal Bando

C. Reggie Jackson

D. Ray Fosse

4. The Philadelphia Athletics won their first-ever World Series title in 1910 and followed it up with two more championship flags in 1911 and 1913. Which A's player had a remarkable stretch of nine hits in each one of those three series?

A. Rube Oldring

B. Bris Lord

C. Eddie Collins

D. Home Run Baker

Singles

1. Which Seattle youngster hooked the AL Rookie of the Year Award in 2022?

A. Ty France

B. Cal Raleigh

C. Julio Rodríguez

D. J. P. Crawford

2. Name the reliever who set the Mariners' single-season team record for saves with 57 lockdowns in 2018.

A. Nick Vincent

B. James Pazos

C. Edwin Díaz

D. Steve Cishek

3. Which Mariners ace won the AL Cy Young Award in 2010 and tossed a perfect game against the Tampa Bay Rays in 2012?

A. James Paxton

B. Randy Johnson

C. Jason Vargas

D. Félix Hernández

4. Which baseball phenom joined the Seattle squad in 2001 and promptly won both the AL Rookie of the Year title and AL MVP Award?

A. Alex Rodriguez

B. Ichiro Suzuki

C. David Bell

D. Bret Boone

Doubles

1. In what year did the Seattle Mariners debut in their first MLB game?

A. 1977

B. 1978

C. 1979

D. 1980

2. Which Hall of Famer and Mariners icon won the AL MVP Award in 1997?

A. Jay Buhner

B. Alex Rodriguez

C. José Cruz

D. Ken Griffey Jr.

3. Hall of Fame pitcher Randy Johnson won his first Cy Young Award with the Mariners in 1995, but what was his win-loss record during that unforgettable campaign?

A. 17–3

B. 18–2

C. 19–2

D. 19–3

4. Which Seattle hitting machine won AL batting titles in both 1992 and 1995?

A. Edgar Martínez

B. Jay Buhner

C. Tino Martinez

D. Mike Blowers

//

Triples

1. All-star Jay Buhner was traded by the New York Yankees to the Mariners in 1988 for which player made famous in *Seinfeld* TV sitcom lore?

A. Henry Cotto

B. Ken Phelps

C. Scott Bradley

D. Steve Balboni

2. Which Seattle hurler led his team with 17 wins in 1984?

A. Mike Moore

B. Matt Young

C. Mark Langston

D. Scott Bankhead

3. Which Mariners mauler harpooned his way to an AL Rookie of the Year Award in 1984?

A. Dave Henderson

B. Jim Presley

C. Spike Owen

D. Alvin Davis

4. Which Seattle player belted four home runs in a single game against the Chicago White Sox on May 2, 2002?

A. Rubén Sierra

B. Bret Boone

C. Mike Cameron

D. Carlos Guillén

Home Runs

1. Which player had the first hit in Mariners history?

A. José Báez

B. Dave Collins

C. Ruppert Jones

D. Craig Reynolds

2. Which player hit the first home run in Mariners history?

A. Juan Bernhardt

B. Bill Stein

C. Steve Braun

D. Carlos López

3. Which pitcher holds the Mariners' single-season team record for wins with 21 victories?

A. Mike Moore

B. Jamie Moyer

C. Erik Hanson

D. Freddy García

4. Which baseburner holds the Mariners' single-season team record for stolen bases with 60 bags snagged?

A. Julio Cruz

B. Brian Hunter

C. Mallex Smith

D. Harold Reynolds

Playoffs / World Series

1. In Game 5 of the 1995 ALDS, which three Mariners batters had consecutive hits in the 11th inning, lifting Seattle to a 6–5 series-clinching victory?

A. Vince Coleman, Ken Griffey Jr., Edgar Martínez

B. Luis Sojo, Jay Buhner, Edgar Martínez

C. Joey Cora, Ken Griffey Jr., Edgar Martínez

D. Dan Wilson, Ken Griffey Jr., Tino Martinez

2. In Game 5 of the 1995 ALDS, which Seattle batter drew a walk against New York Yankees pitcher David Cone in the eighth inning to tie the score at 4–4?

A. Chris Widger

B. Alex Diaz

C. Félix Fermín

D. Doug Strange

3. Which New York Yankees pitcher gave up the walk-off hit to Edgar Martínez in Game 5 of the 1995 ALDS, sending Seattle to its first-ever ALCS?

A. Scott Kamieniecki

B. Jack McDowell

C. Bob Wickman

D. John Wetteland

4. Which Seattle pitcher picked up a save in Game 3 of the 1995 ALDS and then the win in Game 4?

A. Norm Charlton

B. Bobby Ayala

C. Bill Risley

D. Jeff Nelson

Seattle's lovable team mascot, the Mariner Moose, first appeared in 1990 and was portrayed originally by DJ and entertainer Tiger Budbill.

Singles

1. Which flashy Rays player took home the AL Rookie of the Year Award in 2021?

A. Manuel Margot

B. Austin Meadows

C. Brandon Lowe

D. Randy Arozarena

2. Which Tampa Bay hurler netted an AL Cy Young Award in 2018?

A. Chris Archer

B. Tyler Glasnow

C. Jake Faria

D. Blake Snell

3. Name the Rays pitcher who led the AL with 20 wins in 2012—the same season he also claimed the AL Cy Young Award.

A. David Price

B. Matt Moore

C. James Shields

D. Alex Cobb

4. Which talented Tampa Bay youngster tabbed the AL Rookie of the Year Award in 2013?

A. Wil Myers

B. Matt Joyce

C. Luke Scott

D. Desmond Jennings

Doubles

1. In what year did Tampa Bay debut in their first MLB game?

A. 1997

B. 1998

C. 1999

D. 1993

2. In what year did Tampa Bay drop the "Devil" portion of their name and start playing simply as the Rays?

A. 2006

B. 2007

C. 2008

D. 2009

3. Which Rays first-round pick pocketed the AL Rookie of the Year Award in 2008?

A. Gabe Gross

B. B. J. Upton

C. Evan Longoria

D. Jason Bartlett

4. Which Rays pitcher made a splash by winning the AL Rookie of the Year Award in 2011?

A. Wade Davis

B. Jeff Niemann

C. Alex Cobb

D. Jeremy Hellickson

Triples

1. Which Tampa Bay Rays standout was named MVP of the 2009 MLB All-Star Game?

A. Carl Crawford

B. Ben Zobrist

C. Gabe Kapler

D. B. J. Upton

2. Who was the first manager in Tampa Bay history?

A. Frank Howard

B. Larry Rothschild

C. Hal McRae

D. Lou Piniella

3. Which thumper holds the Tampa Bay single-season team record for home runs, with 46 battered bombs?

A. Brandon Lowe

B. Carlos Peña

C. Aubrey Huff

D. Logan Morrison

4. Which pitcher holds the Rays' team record for career wins, with 87 victories in a Tampa Bay uniform?

A. Chris Archer

B. Jake Odorizzi

C. James Shields

D. Scott Kazmir

Home Runs

1. Which player had the first hit in Rays history?

A. Quinton McCracken

B. Miguel Cairo

C. Dave Martinez

D. Mike Kelly

2. Which pitcher recorded the first win in Rays history?

A. Tony Saunders

B. Wilson Álvarez

C. Dennis Springer

D. Rolando Arrojo

3. Which player was selected by Tampa Bay as the first overall pick in the first round of the 1999 MLB June Amateur Draft?

A. Doug Waechter

B. Josh Hamilton

C. Ryan Raburn

D. Seth McClung

4. Name the Hall of Fame player who recorded his 3,000th career hit—a home run—with Tampa Bay in 1999 and who also hit the first home run in Rays history.

A. Wade Boggs

B. Craig Biggio

C. Paul Molitor

D. Fred McGriff

Playoffs / World Series

1. Which Tampa Bay player slugged three home runs in the 2020 ALCS, helping the Rays capture their second AL pennant?

A. Kevin Kiermaier

B. Yandy Díaz

C. Mike Zunino

D. Manuel Margot

2. In the eighth inning of Game 5 of the 2020 ALDS, which Rays player smashed a game-winning home run off New York Yankees reliever Aroldis Chapman?

A. Mike Brosseau

B. Brett Phillips

C. Willy Adames

D. Jiman Choi

3. Which Tampa Bay twirler earned 2008 ALCS MVP honors for his great effort on the mound against the Boston Red Sox?

A. Grant Balfour

B. Andy Sonnanstine

C. Matt Garza

D. Scott Kazmir

4. Which Rays batter delivered a game-winning sacrifice fly in the 11th inning of Game 2 of the 2008 ALCS?

A. Akinori Iwamura

B. B. J. Upton

C. Dioner Navarro

D. Cliff Floyd

The Tampa Bay team name refers to both manta rays and rays of sunshine, both of which are represented on their uniforms.

TEXAS RANGERS

Singles

1. Which Rangers roughhouse player led his squad in home runs in both 2016 and 2019?

A. Prince Fielder

B. Rougned Odor

C. Mitch Moreland

D. Nomar Mazara

2. Name the Texas terror who had back-to-back 40 home runs seasons in 2017–2018.

A. Shin-Soo Choo

B. Elvis Andrus

C. Joey Gallo

D. Danny Santana

3. Which Rangers slugger lassoed both an AL batting title and MVP Award in 2010?

A. Josh Hamilton

B. Ian Kinsler

C. Nelson Cruz

D. Vladimir Guerrero

4. Which Texas all-star won the AL Rookie of the Year Award in 2010?

A. Justin Smoak

B. Tommy Hunter

C. Julio Borbón

D. Neftalí Feliz

Doubles

1. In what year did the Washington Senators move to Texas and become the Rangers?

A. 1970

B. 1971

C. 1972

D. 1973

2. Which Texas thumper stampeded his way to an AL MVP Award in 2003?

A. Hank Blalock

B. Alex Rodriguez

C. Mark Teixeira

D. Rafael Palmeiro

3. Rangers Hall of Fame catcher Iván Rodríguez had a monster year in 1999. What did he accomplish that season?

A. He was an all-star, won a batting title, and was awarded both the Gold Glove and Silver Slugger

B. He was an all-star, won ALCS MVP, and was awarded both the Gold Glove and Silver Slugger

C. He was an all-star, led the AL in home runs, and was awarded both the Gold Glove and Silver Slugger

D. He was an all-star, won AL MVP, and was awarded both the Gold Glove and Silver Slugger

4. Which Rangers megastar roped in two AL MVP Awards in 1996 and 1998?

A. Juan González

B. Will Clark

C. Mickey Tettleton

D. Rusty Greer

///

Triples

1. Texas infielder Michael Young won an AL batting title in 2005. What did he hit that season to secure the top spot?

A. .333

B. .334

C. .339

D. .331

2. The Rangers retired number 29 in honor of which great player in their history?

A. Adrian Beltré

B. Buddy Bell

C. Johnny Oates

D. Nolan Ryan

3. Which terrific Texas hitter rode a hot bat all the way to an AL batting title in 1991?

A. Steve Buechele

B. Julio Franco

C. Rubén Sierra

D. Brian Downing

4. Name the pitcher who holds the Rangers' single-season team record for wins, as well as the number of victories and the year he set the mark.

A. Nolan Ryan, 22 wins in 1991

B. Kevin Brown, 21 wins in 1992

C. Fergie Jenkins, 25 wins in 1974

D. Nolan Ryan, 22 wins in 1990

//

Home Runs

1. How many career hits did Rangers standout Toby Harrah collect during his 17 seasons in the big leagues?

A. 1,954

B. 1,978

C. 1.992

D. 2,013

2. Which Texas youngster blazed a trail by winning the AL Rookie of the Year Award in 1974?

A. Lenny Randle

B. Jim Spencer

C. Jim Sundberg

D. Mike Hargrove

3. Which Texas player two-stepped his way to an AL MVP Award in 1974?

A. Claudell Washington

B. Tom Grieve

C. Jeff Burroughs

D. Willie Horton

4. Name the Texas-sized slugger who twice led the AL in home runs (in 1968 and 1970) while a member of the Washington Senators.

A. Don Lock

B. Frank Howard

C. Jim King

D. Harmon Killebrew

Playoffs / World Series

1. Which Rangers bruiser belted five home runs and had a record-setting 15 RBI in the 2023 ALCS, easily rounding up series MVP honors?

A. Mitch Garver

B. Jonah Heim

C. Adolis García

D. Nathaniel Lowe

2. Which Texas player cracked three home runs in the 2023 World Series and was named MVP of that series?

A. Corey Seager

B. Marcus Semien

C. Josh Jung

D. Evan Carter

3. In Game 2 of the 2011 ALCS, which Rangers player rocked a walk-off grand slam in the 11th inning?

A. David Murphy

B. Nelson Cruz

C. Mitch Moreland

D. Mike Napoli

4. Which Texas pitcher won two games in the 2010 ALCS, including the clincher in Game 6 to send the Rangers to their first-ever World Series?

A. Derek Holland

B. C. J. Wilson

C. Cliff Lee

D. Colby Lewis

Texas pitcher Kenny Rogers tossed a perfect game against the California Angels on July 28, 1994.

TORONTO BLUE JAYS

Singles

1. Which Blue Jays bat man led the AL with 48 home runs in 2021?

A. Alejandro Kirk

B. Vladimir Guerrero Jr.

C. Whit Merrifield

D. Matt Chapman

2. Which Toronto all-star led the AL in hits in both 2021 and 2022?

A. Daulton Varsho

B. Cavan Biggio

C. Bo Bichette

D. George Springer

3. Name the Toronto Blue Bird who flew away with the AL Cy Young Award in 2021.

A. Alek Manaoh

B. Kevin Gausman

C. Robbie Ray

D. José Berríos

4. Which Blue Jays thumper feathered his own nest with an AL MVP Award in 2015?

A. Josh Donaldson

B. Chris Colabello

C. Kevin Pillar

D. Edwin Encarnación

Doubles

1. In what year did the Toronto Blue Jays debut in their first MLB game?

A. 1974
B. 1975
C. 1976
D. 1977

2. Which Toronto pitcher earned an AL Cy Young Award in 2003?

A. Doug Davis
B. Roy Halladay
C. Kelvim Escobar
D. Mark Hendrickson

3. Which Blue Jays nestling netted an AL Rookie of the Year award in 2002?

A. Josh Phelps
B. Shannon Stewart
C. Eric Hinske
D. Vernon Wells

4. Which boisterous bat flipper holds the Blue Jays' single-season team record for home runs, with 54 baseballs flown out of the park?

A. Marcus Semien
B. Carlos Delgado
C. Jose Canseco
D. José Bautista

Triples

1. Which two Blue Jays pitchers combined to win three consecutive AL Cy Young Awards from 1996–1998?

A. Pat Hentgen and Roger Clemens
B. David Wells and Roger Clemens
C. Jack Morris and Roger Clemens
D. J. A. Happ and Roger Clemens

2. Name the Toronto all-star who won the AL batting title in 1993.

A. Joe Carter
B. John Olerud
C. Paul Molitor
D. Roberto Alomar

3. Which Toronto pitcher captured an AL ERA title in 1987?

A. Jim Clancy
B. Jimmy Key
C. John Cerutti
D. Tom Henke

4. Which Blue Jays bomber bashed his way to an AL MVP Award in 1987?

A. Willie Upshaw
B. Fred McGriff
C. Lloyd Moseby
D. George Bell

Home Runs

1. Which player had the first hit—a home run—in Toronto Blue Jays history?

A. John Scott

B. Rick Cerone

C. Doug Ault

D. Otto Vélez

2. Name the Toronto Blue Bird who led the AL with 40 homers in 1986.

A. Lloyd Moseby

B. Cliff Johnson

C. Willie Upshaw

D. Jesse Barfield

3. Which Blue Jays pitcher landed an AL ERA title in 1985?

A. Dave Stieb

B. Dave Stewart

C. Doyle Alexander

D. Dennis Lamp

4. Which Blue Jays chick learned to fly in 1979 by winning the AL Rookie of the Year award?

A. Alfredo Griffin

B. Danny Ainge

C. Dámaso García

D. Phil Huffman

In 1992, Blue Jays skipper Cito Gaston became the first Black manager in MLB history to win a World Series title.

Playoffs / World Series

1. Which Blue Jays legendary hero hit a walk-off home run in Game 6 of the 1993 World Series?

A. Rickey Henderson

B. Joe Carter

C. Ed Sprague

D. Devon White

2. Which Toronto player took home the 1993 World Series MVP Award for his exceptional hitting against the Philadelphia Phillies?

A. Paul Molitor

B. Rickey Henderson

C. Roberto Alomar

D. Tony Fernández

3. In Game 6 of the 1992 World Series, which Blue Jays batter delivered the game-winning hit in the 11th inning to secure Toronto's first-ever world championship?

A. Kelly Gruber

B. Roberto Alomar

C. Devon White

D. Dave Winfield

4. Which Blue Jays player was named MVP of the 1992 World Series for his fine overall performance?

A. Roberto Alomar

B. Rance Mulliniks

C. Pat Borders

D. Candy Maldonado

Answers: Singles: 1. B, 2. C, 3. C, 4. A; Doubles: 1. D, 2. B, 3. C, 4. D; Triples: 1. A, 2. B, 3. B, 4. D; Home Runs: 1. C, 2. D, 3. A, 4. A; Playoffs/World Series: 1. B, 2. A, 3. D, 4. C

NATIONAL
League

ARIZONA DIAMONDBACKS

Singles

1. Which Diamondbacks baby rattler nabbed the NL Rookie of the Year Award in 2023?

A. Gabriel Moreno

B. Zac Gallen

C. Geraldo Perdomo

D. Corbin Carroll

2. Which hurler won 21 games for the Diamondbacks in 2011, the season when the team led the NL?

A. Ian Kennedy

B. Daniel Hudson

C. Randy Johnson

D. Brandon Webb

3. Who was the first manager in Arizona Diamondbacks history?

A. Bob Brenly

B. Bob Melvin

C. Buck Showalter

D. Kirk Gibson

4. Which first baseman won four NL Silver Slugger Awards for the Diamondbacks from 2013–2018?

A. Mark Grace

B. Paul Goldschmidt

C. Adam LaRoche

D. Mark Reynolds

Doubles

1. In what year did the Arizona Diamondbacks debut in their first MLB game?

A. 1999

B. 1998

C. 1887

D. 1991

2. Which slugger led the Diamondbacks in both home runs and runs batted in (RBI) in 2019, clocking 35 dingers and driving in 118 runs?

A. Christian Walker

B. Adam Jones

C. Eduardo Escobar

D. Ketel Marte

3. Which Diamondbacks player led the NL in hits in 2016 with 203 knocks?

A. Brandon Drury

B. Jake Lamb

C. Nick Ahmed

D. Jean Segura

4. Former Diamondbacks shortstop Didi Gregorius was born in which country?

A. Bermuda (UK)

B. Haiti

C. The Dominican Republic

D. The Netherlands

Triples

1. Which unlucky Diamondbacks batter was hit by a pitch (HBP) a single-season team record 22 times in 2019?

A. Carson Kelly

B. Tim Locastro

C. Tony Womack

D. Wilmer Flores

2. Name the Arizona outfielder who led the team with 22 stolen bases in their inaugural season.

A. Brent Brede

B. David Dellucci

C. Devon White

D. Karim García

3. Which star set the Arizona Diamondbacks single-season team record for runs scored in 1999 with a whopping 132?

A. Jay Bell

B. Matt Williams

C. Luis Gonzalez

D. Steve Finley

4. Which Arizona hurler had the honor of being the Opening Day starter for the Snakes back in 2010?

A. Dan Haren

B. Wade Miley

C. Javier Vázquez

D. Madison Bumgarner

Home Runs

1. Which reliever holds the Arizona Diamondbacks single-season team record for saves with 47 and in what year did he accomplish this remarkable feat?

A. J. J. Putz in 2011

B. Fernando Rodney in 2017

C. José Valverde in 2007

D. J. J. Putz in 2012

2. Which Arizona infielder led the team in 2004 with a .310 batting average?

A. Alex Cintrón

B. Danny Bautista

C. Roberto Alomar

D. Shea Hillenbrand

3. Which player delivered the first hit in Arizona Diamondbacks history?

A. David Dellucci

B. Travis Lee

C. Andy Fox

D. Karim Garcia

4. Who was the first player ever drafted by the Arizona Diamondbacks?

A. Nick Bierbrodt

B. Jack Cust

C. Carlos Quentin

D. Stephen Drew

Playoffs / World Series

1. In the ninth inning of Game 7 of the 2001 World Series, which Diamondbacks hero had the game-winning (and championship-winning) hit against the New York Yankees?

A. Matt Williams

B. Tony Womack

C. Jay Bell

D. Luis Gonzalez

2. In that same 2001 World Series, which D-backs pitcher was credited with wins in both Game 6 and Game 7?

A. Brian Anderson

B. Byung-Hyun Kim

C. Randy Johnson

D. Miguel Batista

3. In that same 2001 World Series, which Arizona player scored the tying run in the ninth inning of Game 7 to knot the score at 2–2?

A. Midre Cummings

B. Damian Miller

C. Craig Counsell

D. Mark Grace

4. In that same 2001 World Series, Tony Womack's double in the ninth inning of Game 7 drove in the run for Arizona that tied the score at 2-2. What was the count when he delivered his clutch hit and who was the home plate umpire?

A. 1-2 count, home plate umpire Dale Scott

B. 2-2 count, home plate umpire Steve Rippley

C. 0-2 count, home plate umpire Jim Joyce

D. 3-2 count, home plate umpire Dana DeMuth

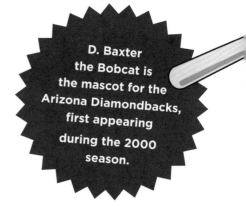

D. Baxter the Bobcat is the mascot for the Arizona Diamondbacks, first appearing during the 2000 season.

Atlanta Braves

Singles

1. In 2023, which Braves star became the first player ever to hit 40 or more home runs in a season while also stealing 70 or more bases in that same campaign?

A. Ozzie Albies

B. Ron Gant

C. Ronald Acuña Jr.

D. David Justice

2. Name the Atlanta thumper who slugged a staggering 54 home runs in 2023 along with 139 RBI, which both led the NL.

A. Marcell Ozuna

B. Orlando Arcia

C. Austin Riley

D. Matt Olson

3. Which Braves phenom took home NL Rookie of the Year honors in 2022?

A. Spencer Strider

B. Michael Harris II

C. Max Fried

D. Vaughn Grissom

4. Which Atlanta pitcher totaled 37 saves in 2021, helping the Braves to a World Series title?

A. Raisel Iglesias

B. Will Smith

C. A. J. Minter

D. Mark Wohlers

///

Doubles

1. In what year did the Braves move from Milwaukee to Atlanta?

A. 1966

B. 1965

C. 1969

D. 1968

2. The Atlanta Braves retired uniform number 3 in honor of which great player from their team history?

A. Chipper Jones

B. Warren Spahn

C. John Smoltz

D. Dale Murphy

3. The 1982 Atlanta Braves were an exciting club that won the NL West crown, marking their first playoff appearance since 1969. Which pitcher on that squad led the team with 17 wins that season?

A. Gene Garber

B. Rick Mahler

C. Phil Niekro

D. Rick Camp

4. Which Braves player smacked four home runs in a single game against the Montreal Expos on July 6, 1986, despite the fact that his team still lost?

A. Bob Horner

B. Claudell Washington

C. Ozzie Virgil

D. Ken Oberkfell

Triples

1. The Braves went from worst to first in 1991, advancing all the way to the World Series. Which player on that team electrified the fans by swiping 72 stolen bases?

A. Ron Gant

B. Otis Nixon

C. Deion Sanders

D. Brian Hunter

2. The resurgence of the Braves in 1991 was due in large part to which great player who took home NL MVP honors that season?

A. Fred McGriff

B. Sid Bream

C. Terry Pendleton

D. Jeff Blauser

3. Which talented player helped lay the foundation for that great Braves run in 1991 by winning the NL Rookie of the Year Award in 1990?

A. Ron Gant

B. Steve Avery

C. Tom Glavine

D. David Justice

1. How many complete games did Greg Maddux have between 1992 and 1995?
A. 38
B. 37
C. 45
D. 41

//

Home Runs

1. The great Hank Aaron hit a momentous 755 career home runs, nearly all of them in a Braves uniform. Which pitcher surrendered Aaron's first long ball?
A. Bob Gibson
B. Paul Minner
C. Art Fowler
D. Vic Raschi

2. Bobby Cox is the winningest manager in Braves team history, with a record of 2149–1709. Who is second on that list, with a record of 1004–649?
A. Joe Torre
B. Frank Selee
C. Casey Stengel
D. Bill McKechnie

3. Who did Atlanta take as the first overall pick in the first round of the 1990 MLB June Amateur Draft?
A. Chipper Jones
B. Ryan Klesko
C. Mike Kelly
D. Steve Avery

4. Which player holds the Braves team record for most career triples with 103?
A. Herman Long
B. Hugh Duffy
C. Rabbit Maranville
D. Bill Bruton

//

Playoffs / World Series

1. Which super-clutch Braves hero delivered the walk-off hit in Game 7 of the 1992 National League Championship Series (NLCS) against the Pittsburgh Pirates, sending Atlanta to the World Series for the second year in a row?
A. Mark Lemke
B. Rafael Belliard
C. Damon Berryhill
D. Francisco Cabrera

2. Name the Braves slugger who cracked home runs in three consecutive games during the 1995 World Series against Cleveland.

A. Marquis Grissom

B. Mike Devereaux

C. Ryan Klesko

D. Javy López

3. Which Houston Astros batter grounded out against Atlanta closer Will Smith, ending the 2021 World Series and giving the Atlanta Braves their second world championship?

A. Michael Brantley

B. Alex Bregman

C. Yuli Gurriel

D. Jose Altuve

The Braves introduced "the Freeze" in 2017, allowing fans a chance to see if they could outrace the fleet-footed phenom.

4. Which Braves pitcher shut down the vaunted New York Yankees lineup in Game 7 of the 1957 World Series, giving the Braves their only World Series title while in Milwaukee?

A. Warren Spahn

B. Lew Burdette

C. Bob Buhl

D. Gene Conley

CHICAGO CUBS

Singles

1. The Chicago Cubs play home games at Wrigley Field, one of the best venues to watch a ballgame. When did that grand old landmark first open its doors?

A. 1912
B. 1913
C. 1914
D. 1916

2. What is the street address for Wrigley Field?

A. 1060 West Addison Street
B. 1160 West Addison Street
C. 1060 East Addison Street
D. 1260 Sandberg Street

3. Which Cubs hurler snagged 16 victories in 2023, earning a spot on the NL All-Star team?

A. Drew Smyly
B. Marcus Stroman
C. Kyle Hendricks
D. Justin Steele

4. Name the Cubs legend who debuted in 1953 and became known for his famous catchphrase, "Let's play two!"

A. Andre Dawson
B. Ernie Banks
C. Ron Santo
D. Mike Ditka

Doubles

1. Which Hall of Fame Cubbie earned NL MVP honors in 1984, leading the NL in runs scored and triples?

A. Jody Davis
B. Leon Durham
C. Keith Moreland
D. Ryne Sandberg

2. The game that occurred on June 23, 1984 is known in Cubs folklore as "the Sandberg Game." Which St. Louis Cardinals pitcher did Ryne Sandberg homer off of twice in the late innings to help propel the Cubs to an impossible victory?

A. Danny Cox
B. Todd Worrell
C. Bruce Sutter
D. John Tudor

3. Which Chicago outfielder won the NL Rookie of the Year Award in 1989 after helping the Cubs secure the NL East crown?

A. Dwight Smith
B. Doug Dascenzo
C. Jerome Walton
D. Shawon Dunston

CHICAGO CUBS

4. Which Chicago Cubs clubber had a monster season in 1987, easily taking home the NL MVP Award?

A. Andre Dawson

B. Rafael Palmeiro

C. Mark Grace

D. Gary Matthews

//

Triples

1. Sammy Sosa led the Cubs in 1998 with a whopping 66 home runs, but who was second on the team (with a respectable 31 deep flies)?

A. José Hernández

B. Henry Rodríguez

C. Brant Brown

D. Mark Grace

2. Flamethrower Kerry Wood had a game for the ages on May 6, 1998 against the Houston Astros. How many strikeouts did he rack up and who was the final batter that he fanned?

A. 20 strikeouts, final batter Craig Biggio

B. 20 strikeouts, final batter Dave Clark

C. 21 strikeouts, final batter Brad Ausmus

D. 20 strikeouts, final batter Derek Bell

3. Which Cubs pitcher won the NL Cy Young Award in 1971 with 24 wins and 30 complete games?

A. Fergie Jenkins

B. Milt Pappas

C. Burt Hooton

D. Rick Reuschel

4. Which Cubs icon debuted in 1960 (going on to win five Gold Glove Awards and earn nine NL All-Star appearances) and what number did Chicago retire in his honor?

A. Ernie Banks, retired number 14

B. Ron Santo, retired number 10

C. Ernie Banks, retired number 12

D. Ron Santo, retired number 15

//

Home Runs

1. Which Cubs great grabbed the NL Rookie of the Year Award in 1961, hitting 25 home runs and driving in 86 baserunners?

A. Richie Ashburn

B. Don Zimmer

C. Billy Williams

D. Lee Walls

2. Hack Wilson holds the Chicago Cubs single-season team record—and MLB record—for most RBI in a lone campaign. What year did he set the record and how many batters did he drive in that season?

A. 1929 with 190 RBI

B. 1931 with 192 RBI

C. 1928 with 190 RBI

D. 1930 with 191 RBI

3. "Baseball's Sad Lexicon" is a poem penned in 1910 which details the famous double-play trio for the Chicago Cubs. What are the surnames of the three ballplayers immortalized in both song and verse?

A. Tinker to Evers to Chance

B. Tinker to Allen to Chance

C. Tinker to Evers to Vance

D. Winker to Evers to Chance

4. Which infielder set the Cubs single-season team record for doubles in both 1935 and 1936, and how many doubles did he have in those two campaigns?

A. Rogers Hornsby, 58 doubles in each season

B. Kiki Cuyler, 57 doubles in each season

C. Billy Herman, 57 doubles in each season

D. Rogers Hornsby, 56 doubles in each season

Playoffs/ World Series

1. Which Cubs player took home World Series MVP honors in 2016 after leading his squad to victory over Cleveland?

A. Jon Lester

B. Ben Zobrist

C. Javier Báez

D. Jake Arrieta

2. Which Cubs pitcher surrendered Babe Ruth's famous "Called Shot" home run in Game 3 of the 1932 World Series?

A. Guy Bush

B. Pat Malone

C. Carl Hubbell

D. Charlie Root

3. Name the Chicago pitching ace whose shutout in Game 5 of the 1907 World Series against the Detroit Tigers gave the Cubs their first-ever world title.

A. Mordecai Brown

B. Jack Pfiester

C. Orval Overall

D. Carl Lundgren

4. The Cubs beat the Tigers again in the 1908 World Series. Only one home run was hit in that entire series. Who hit it?

A. Sam Crawford

B. Joe Tinker

C. Ty Cobb

D. Solly Hofman

Before settling on "Cubs," Chicago previously played as the White Stockings, Colts, and Orphans.

Answers: Singles: 1. C, 2. A, 3. D, 4. B; Doubles: 1. D, 2. C, 3. C, 4. A; Triples: 1. B, 2. D, 3. A, 4. B; Home Runs: 1. C, 2. D, 3. A, 4. C; Playoffs/World Series: 1. B, 2. D, 3. A, 4. B

CINCINNATI REDS

Singles

1. What is the name of the venue in which the Cincinnati Reds play their home games currently?

A. Cinergy Field

B. Great American Ball Park

C. Riverfront Stadium

D. Queen City Park

2. Which Reds great won the NL MVP Award in 2010, batting .324 with 37 homers and 113 RBI?

A. Jay Bruce

B. Scott Rolen

C. Joey Votto

D. Nick Castellanos

3. Which Cincinnati pitcher totaled 20 wins for the Reds in 2014 and also led the NL with 242 strikeouts?

A. Johnny Cueto

B. Homer Bailey

C. Mike Leake

D. Tony Cingrani

4. Which Reds reliever tallied 30 or more saves in four consecutive seasons from 2012–2015?

A. Sean Marshall

B. Jonathan Broxton

C. Francisco Cordero

D. Aroldis Chapman

Doubles

1. Which Hall of Fame Cincinnati-born Reds infielder took home the NL MVP trophy in 1995?

A. Hal Morris

B. Barry Larkin

C. Mariano Ducan

D. Todd Benzinger

2. The Cincinnati Reds retired number 10 in honor of which Hall of Fame manager?

A. Sparky Anderson

B. Noodles Hahn

C. Frank Dwyer

D. Clark Griffith

3. How many hits did Cincinnati-born Reds NL MVP Pete Rose record during his 24 seasons in the big leagues?

A. 4,256

B. 4,258

C. 4,252

D. 4,255

4. Which Reds superstar earned NL Rookie of the Year honors in 1968 and was NL MVP in both 1970 and 1972?

A. Ray Knight

B. Johnny Bench

C. Joe Morgan

D. Frank Robinson

Triples

1. Which Cincinnati player notched the NL Rookie of the Year Award in 1988 and was a big part of the Reds 1990 World Series championship?

A. Hal Morris

B. José Rijo

C. Chirs Sabo

D. Kal Daniels

2. Which Reds outfielder cranked 52 home runs in 1977, earning him the NL MVP Award?

A. George Foster

B. César Gerónimo

C. Ken Griffey Jr.

D. Paul O'Neill

3. Which Cincinnati phenom swatted 27 home runs in 1986 (to go along with his 80 stolen bases)?

A. Dave Parker

B. Nick Esasky

C. Eric Davis

D. Dave Collins

4. Which Hall of Famer played 16 of his 23 seasons with the Reds, launching 379 home runs and collecting 2,732 career hits?

A. Tommy Harper

B. Tony Pérez

C. Lee May

D. Ted Kluszewski

Home Runs

1. Which Reds All-Star led the NL in hits in both 1961 and 1963?

A. Wally Post

B. Gus Bell

C. Vada Pinson

D. Tony Oliva

2. The city of Cincinnati is credited with having the first truly all-professional baseball team. In what year did that squad first take the field?

A. 1866

B. 1879

C. 1882

D. 1869

3. Which player holds the Cincinnati Reds single-season team record for batting average with a lofty .377 posting?

A. Edd Roush

B. Ernie Lombardi

C. Cy Seymour

D. Elmer Smith

4. Which pitcher holds the Cincinnati Reds single-season team record for most strikeouts with an amazing 274 Ks?

A. Mario Soto

B. Tom Seaver

C. Jim Maloney

D. Tony Mullane

Playoffs / World Series

1. In Game 7 of the 1975 World Series against the Boston Red Sox, which Reds hero drove in the go-ahead run in the ninth inning to give Cincinnati a 4–3 victory?

A. Pete Rose

B. Ken Griffey Jr.

C. Dave Concepción

D. Joe Morgan

2. In that same Game 7 of the 1975 World Series, which Cincinnati pitcher came on in the bottom of the ninth to earn a save and clinch the flag for the Reds?

A. Will McEnaney

B. Clay Carroll

C. Pat Darcy

D. Pedro Borbón

Hall of Fame hurler Eppa Rixey holds the record for most career wins by a Cincinnati pitcher, tallying 179 wins for the Reds from 1921–1933.

3. Which Reds pitcher spun a complete game gem in Game 7 of the 1940 World Series against the Detroit Tigers, earning Cincinnati their second-ever title flag?

A. Bucky Walters

B. Paul Derringer

C. Don Gullett

D. Johnny Vander Meer

4. The Cincinnati Reds won their first-ever World Series title in 1919 against the infamous "Chicago Black Sox." Which Reds player collected 10 hits in that series?

A. Pat Duncan

B. Heinie Groh

C. Greasy Neale

D. Morrie Rath

CINCINNATI REDS

134

Answers: Singles: 1. B, 2. C, 3. A, 4. D; Doubles: 1. B, 2. A, 3. A, 4. B; Triples: 1. C, 2. A, 3. C, 4. B; Home Runs: 1. C, 2. D, 3. C, 4. A; Playoffs/World Series: 1. D, 2. A, 3. B, 4. C

COLORADO ROCKIES

Singles

1. Which Colorado Rockies rookie smacked 24 homers and had 99 RBI in 2007?

A. Brad Hawpe

B. Garrett Atkins

C. Troy Tulowitzki

D. Ryan Spilborghs

2. Which Colorado kingpin led the NL in homers and RBI in both 2015 and 2016?

A. Mark Reynolds

B. DJ LeMahieu

C. Carlos González

D. Nolan Arenado

3. In 2017, which Rockies player led the NL in hits, triples, runs scored, and batting average?

A. DJ LeMahieu

B. Charlie Blackmon

C. Gerardo Parra

D. Ian Desmond

4. Which pitcher led the Rockies with 17 victories in 2018?

A. Germán Márquez

B. Kyle Freeland

C. Jon Gray

D. Tyler Chatwood

Doubles

1. In what year did the Colorado Rockies debut in their first MLB game?

A. 1992

B. 1993

C. 1990

D. 1991

2. What colorful nickname was given to the Colorado Rockies of the 1990s?

A. The Roughhouse Rockers

B. The Colorado Clouters

C. The Blake Street Bombers

D. The Rocky Mountain Rollers

3. Which Rockies player led the NL with a .372 batting average in 2000?

A. Jeff Cirillo

B. Ellis Burks

C. Jeffrey Hammonds

D. Todd Helton

4. Which Colorado clubber captured NL MVP honors in 1997?

A. Larry Walker

B. Juan Pierre

C. Dante Bichette

D. Quinton McCracken

Triples

1. Who was the first manager in the history of the Colorado Rockies?

A. Don Baylor

B. Walt Weiss

C. Clint Hurdle

D. Buddy Bell

2. Who was the speedster who nabbed 68 stolen bases in 2008, setting a Colorado Rockies single season team record?

A. Juan Pierre

B. Eric Young Sr.

C. Willy Taveras

D. Tom Goodwin

3. Which Colorado thumper led the NL in hits, doubles, RBI, and batting average in 2007?

A. Trevor Story

B. Ryan McMahon

C. Matt Holliday

D. Ellis Burks

4. Which Rockies player led the NL in both hits and batting average in 2010?

A. Dexter Fowler

B. Brad Hawpe

C. Aaron Miles

D. Carlos González

Home Runs

1. From which country does former Rockies pitching great Ubaldo Jiménez hail?

A. Puerto Rico

B. The Dominican Republic

C. Cuba

D. Venezuela

2. Rockies standout Vinny Castilla made his MLB debut with a different team. Which squad was it?

1. Atlanta Braves

2. Pittsburgh Pirates

3. Chicago Cubs

4. Toronto Blue Jays

3. Which Colorado hitting machine had an all-time season in 1996, leading the NL with 47 homers and 150 RBI?

A. Ellis Burks

B. Dante Bichette

C. Andrés Galarraga

D. Todd Helton

4. Which Rockies Gold Glover led the NL in triples in 1999?

A. Cory Sullivan

B. Tyler Colvin

C. Dexter Fowler

D. Neifi Pérez

Playoffs / World Series

1. Which team did the Colorado Rockies sweep in the 2007 NLCS to advance to their first World Series?

A. San Diego Padres

B. Arizona Diamondbacks

C. Cincinnati Reds

D. Philadelphia Phillies

2. Which Rockies pitcher had a win and two saves in that same 2007 NLCS?

A. Jeff Francis

B. Brian Fuentes

C. Manny Corpas

D. LaTroy Hawkins

3. Which Colorado hurler picked up the win in Game 3 of the 1995 National League Division Series (NLDS) against the Atlanta Braves?

A. Darren Holmes

B. Lance Painter

C. Mark Thompson

D. Curt Leskanic

4. The Rockies beat the San Francisco Giants to secure the first-ever NL Wild Card in 1995. What was the final score of that memorable game?

A. 10-8

B. 10-9

C. 5-4

D. 6-3

The Rockies played home games at Mile High Stadium during their first two seasons before moving to the newly built Coors Field.

LOS ANGELES *Dodgers*

Singles

1. Which Dodgers pitching legend won both the NL Cy Young and MVP Awards in 2014, as well as two previous NL Cy Young Awards in 2011 and 2013?

A. Dan Haren

B. Josh Beckett

C. Clayton Kershaw

D. Zack Greinke

2. Which all-star smacked 39 homers and drove in 107 runs for the Dodgers in 2023?

A. Mookie Betts

B. Max Muncy

C. James Outman

D. J. D. Martinez

3. Name the Dodgers slugger who led the NL in doubles with a whopping 59 two-baggers in 2023.

A. Jason Heyward

B. Chris Taylor

C. Will Smith

D. Freddie Freeman

4. Which baseball legend has had his number 42 retired by not only the Dodgers but all of Major League Baseball?

A. Jim Gilliam

B. Jackie Robinson

C. Brickyard Kennedy

D. Zack Wheat

Doubles

1. In what year did the Dodgers move from Brooklyn to Los Angeles?

A. 1958

B. 1957

C. 1959

D. 1956

2. Which Dodgers pitcher had 59 consecutive scoreless innings in 1988—a magical season in which he captured the NL Cy Young Award?

A. Tim Leary

B. Jay Howell

C. Orel Hershiser

D. Don Sutton

3. Name the Dodgers pitcher who won both the NL Rookie of the Year and Cy Young Awards in 1981, setting off a "mania" in Los Angeles.

A. Dave Stewart

B. Burt Hooton

C. Bob Welch

D. Fernando Valenzuela

4. Which five Dodgers players won the NL Rookie of the Year Award in consecutive seasons from 1992–1996?

A. José Offerman (1992), Mike Piazza (1993), Raúl Mondesi (1994), Hideo Nomo (1995), Todd Hollandsworth (1996)

B. Eric Karros (1992), Mike Piazza (1993), Tom Goodwin (1994), Hideo Nomo (1995), Todd Hollandsworth (1996)

C. Eric Karros (1992), Mike Piazza (1993), Raúl Mondesi (1994), Hideo Nomo (1995), Todd Hollandsworth (1996)

D. Eric Karros (1992), Mike Piazza (1993), Raúl Mondesi (1994), Hideo Nomo (1995), Lenny Harris (1996)

Triples

1. Which Los Angeles Dodgers standout earned NL MVP honors in 1974?

A. Dusty Baker

B. Steve Garvey

C. Ron Cey

D. Davey Lopes

2. Who is the winningest manager in Dodgers history, with 2,040 victories?

A. Walter Alston

B. Casey Stengel

C. Tommy Lasorda

D. Leo Durocher

3. Which Brooklyn Dodgers bomber led the NL with 43 home runs in 1956?

A. Sandy Amorós

B. Duke Snider

C. Carl Furillo

D. Gil Hodges

4. Name the Dodgers ace who won both the NL Cy Young and MVP Awards in 1963, as well as additional NL Cy Young Awards in 1965 and 1966.

A. Don Drysdale

B. Claude Osteen

C. Don Newcombe

D. Sandy Koufax

Home Runs

1. The Dodgers have retired number 1 in honor of which Hall of Fame player?

A. Gil Hodges

B. Jim Gilliam

C. Pee Wee Reese

D. Tommy Lasorda

2. Which Dodgers pitching powerhouse led the NL with 25 wins in 1962, earning him the NL Cy Young Award that season?

A. Johnny Podres

B. Carl Erskine

C. Don Drysdale

D. Sal Maglie

3. Which Brooklyn Dodgers Hall of Famer won three NL MVP Awards in 1951, 1953, and 1955?

A. Roy Campanella

B. Jackie Robinson

C. Duke Snider

D. Rube Walker

4. Which Dodgers hurler was the NL Rookie of the Year in 1949 and also won the NL Cy Young and MVP Awards in 1956?

A. Carl Erskine

B. Don Newcombe

C. Roger Craig

D. Clem Labine

Playoffs / World Series

1. Which Dodgers player took home MVP honors for his great play in the 2020 World Series against the Tampa Bay Rays?

A. Walker Buehler

B. Joc Pederson

C. Max Muncy

D. Corey Seager

2. In Game 1 of the 1988 World Series, which Dodgers player smacked an unforgettable ninth inning home run, lifting Los Angeles to an impossible 5–4 victory?

A. Mike Davis

B. Kirk Gibson

C. Mickey Hatcher

D. Mike Marshall

3. Whose fine performance earned them an MVP Award in the 1959 fall classic against the Chicago White Sox?

A. Johnny Klippstein

B. Chuck Churn

C. Clem Labine

D. Larry Sherry

4. Name the Brooklyn pitcher who shut down the New York Yankees in Game 7 of the 1955 World Series, allowing the Dodgers to clinch their first-ever MLB championship.

A. Johnny Podres

B. Karl Spooner

C. Carl Erskine

D. Clem Labine

The Dodgers were known as the Brooklyn Bridegrooms back in 1889 and played as the Brooklyn Superbas in 1899.

Miami Marlins

Singles

1. Which Marlins pitcher dominated batters in 2022, capturing the NL Cy Young Award?

A. Pablo López

B. Jesús Luzardo

C. Trevor Rogers

D. Sandy Alcántara

2. From what country does Miami all-star Jazz Chisholm Jr. hail?

A. Bahamas

B. Jamaica

C. The Dominican Republic

D. Aruba

3. Who managed the Marlins in 2020 when they made their unlikely playoff run?

A. Fredi González

B. Don Mattingly

C. Skip Schumaker

D. Mike Redmond

4. Which 2017 NL MVP holds the Marlins single-season team record for home runs with 59 round-trippers?

A. Carlos Delgado

B. Jorge Soler

C. Giancarlo Stanton

D. Dan Uggla

Doubles

1. The organization debuted in 1993, but in what year did the Florida Marlins change their name to the Miami Marlins?

A. 2006

B. 2012

C. 2011

D. 2009

2. Which Marlins youngster took home NL Rookie of the Year honors in 2003?

A. Juan Pierre

B. Josh Beckett

C. Miguel Cabrera

D. Dontrelle Willis

3. Which flying Fish led the NL in stolen bases in both 2000 and 2002?

A. Álex González

B. Luis Castillo

C. Juan Pierre

D. Juan Encarnación

4. Which player holds the Marlins single-season team record for batting average with an impressive .354 posting?

A. Miguel Cabrera

B. Chris Coghlan

C. Luis Arráez

D. Dee Strange-Gordon

Triples

1. Which Florida slugger captured the NL Rookie of the Year Award in 2006 and led the NL in batting average in 2009?

A. Hanley Ramírez

B. Dan Uggla

C. Josh Willingham

D. Jeremy Hermida

2. Which Marlins reliever had back-to-back 35-save seasons in 1996 and 1997?

A. Matt Mantei

B. Antonio Alfonseca

C. Robb Nen

D. Kevin Gregg

3. Which Marlins thumper led the team with 31 homers and 103 RBI in 2001?

A. Mike Lowell

B. Derrek Lee

C. Kevin Millar

D. Cliff Floyd

4. How many home runs did superstar Gary Sheffield hit during his productive time with the Marlins?

A. 134

B. 141

C. 122

D. 202

Home Runs

1. Name the player who recorded the first hit in Marlins franchise history.

A. Scott Pose

B. Bret Barberie

C. Junior Félix

D. Orestes Destrade

2. Which Marlins pitcher tossed a no-hitter against the San Diego Padres on May 12, 2001?

A. A.J. Burnett

B. Josh Johnson

C. Ryan Dempster

D. Aníbal Sánchez

3. Which Marlins pitcher won the NL ERA title in 1996 while also leading the staff with 17 victories?

A. Pat Rapp

B. John Burkett

C. Al Leiter

D. Kevin Brown

4. Which Florida fan favorite was nicknamed "Mr. Marlin" due to his significant history with the organization?

A. Jeff Conine

B. Chuck Carr

C. Kurt Abbott

D. Rene Lachemann

Playoffs / World Series

1. How many runs did the Marlins score in the eighth inning of Game 6 of the 2003 NLCS, shocking the Cubs and turning the tide of the series in their favor?

A. 6

B. 7

C. 8

D. 9

2. Name the Marlins player who socked a 12th inning, walk-off home run in Game 4 of the 2003 World Series.

A. Iván Rodríguez

B. Álex González

C. Derrek Lee

D. Miguel Cabrera

Kim Ng was hired as the Miami Marlins general manager in 2020, becoming the first woman GM of a men's team in the history of major North American sports.

MIAMI MARLINS

151

3. In Game 7 of the 1997 World Series, which Marlins player had a sacrifice fly in the ninth inning to tie the score at 2–2?

A. Moisés Alou

B. Bobby Bonilla

C. Charles Johnson

D. Craig Counsell

4. In Game 7 of the 1997 World Series, which Marlins all-time hero had a walk-off single in the 11th inning, capturing the first-ever championship for the Fighting Fish?

A. Édgar Rentería

B. Charles Johnson

C. Darren Daulton

D. Gregg Zaun

Answers: Singles: 1. D, 2. A, 3. B, 4. C; Doubles: 1. B, 2. D, 3. B, 4. C; Triples: 1. A, 2. C, 3. D, 4. C; Home Runs: 1. B, 2. A, 3. D, 4. A; Playoffs/World Series: 1. C, 2. B, 3. D, 4. A

MILWAUKEE BREWERS

Singles

1. Which Brewers standout won the NL MVP Award in 2018, his first season with Milwaukee?

A. Jesús Aguilar

B. Travis Shaw

C. Lorenzo Cain

D. Christian Yelich

2. Name the Milwaukee pitcher who took home the NL Cy Young Award in 2021.

A. Adrian Houser

B. Brandon Woodruff

C. Corbin Burnes

D. Freddy Peralta

3. Which Brewers pitcher notched 34 saves in 2021 to go along with an insane 1.23 ERA?

A. Devin Williams

B. Josh Hader

C. Brad Boxberger

D. Hunter Strickland

4. Which slugger holds the Milwaukee Brewers single-season team record for home runs with 50 moonshots?

A. Prince Fielder

B. Chris Carter

C. Jonathan Lucroy

D. Richie Sexson

Doubles

1. In what year did the Brewers move from the American League to the National League?

A. 1995

B. 1996

C. 1998

D. 1999

2. Which Brewers legend was both the NL Rookie of the Year in 2007 and NL MVP in 2011?

A. Rickie Weeks

B. Ryan Braun

C. Casey McGehee

D. Corey Hart

3. Which Brewers bomber led the team with 34 home runs in 2000?

A. Richie Sexson

B. José Hernández

C. Geoff Jenkins

D. Jeromy Burnitz

4. Which fine Milwaukee hitter led the Brew Crew with a .326 batting average in 1999?

A. Marquis Grissom

B. Mark Loretta

C. Dave Nilsson

D. Jeff Cirillo

Triples

1. Which all-time Brewers great earned AL MVP honors in both 1982 and 1989?

A. Robin Yount

B. Ted Simmons

C. Paul Molitor

D. Don Money

2. How many hits did Milwaukee all-star Paul Molitor collect during his 21-year career?

A. 3,003

B. 3,319

C. 3,120

D. 3,296

3. Which fabulous Brewers batter led the AL in RBI in both 1980 and 1983?

A. Cecil Cooper

B. Rick Manning

C. Ted Simmons

D. Ned Yost

4. Which Milwaukee player led the AL with 41 home runs in 1980?

A. Don Money

B. Ted Simmons

C. Sixto Lezcano

D. Ben Oglivie

Home Runs

1. Name the Milwaukee mauler who led the AL in home runs in both 1979 and 1982.

A. Sal Bando

B. Rob Deer

C. Gorman Thomas

D. Dick Davis

2. Which Brewers pitcher had a standout season in 1986, collecting 20 wins with a 2.79 ERA?

A. Dan Plesac

B. Juan Nieves

C. Mark Clear

D. Teddy Higuera

3. Which Milwaukee player hit a walk-off home run against the Texas Rangers on April 19, 1987, giving the Brewers a blistering 12–0 start to the season?

A. Jim Gantner

B. Dale Sveum

C. Rob Deer

D. Glenn Braggs

4. Who managed the Milwaukee Brewers to their first-ever AL pennant in 1982?

A. Harvey Kuenn

B. Tom Trebelhorn

C. George Bamberger

D. Buck Rodgers

The Milwaukee Brewers started out as the Seattle Pilots in 1969, though they played just one season in the Pacific Northwest.

Playoffs / World Series

1. Which Milwaukee player delivered the walk-off hit in the 10th inning of Game 1 of the 2018 NLDS?

A. Orlando Arcia

B. Mike Moustakas

C. Manny Piña

D. Travis Shaw

2. In the 10th inning of Game 5 of the 2011 NLDS, which Brewers batter came through with a clutch walk-off hit to win them the series against the Arizona Diamondbacks?

A. Nyjer Morgan

B. Jerry Hairston

C. Carlos Gómez

D. Yovani Gallardo

3. Which all-star was named MVP of the 1982 ALCS?

A. Moose Haas

B. Jim Gantner

C. Pete Vuckovich

D. Fred Lynn

4. Which Brewers pitcher tossed a shutout in Game 1 of the 1982 World Series and earned a second victory with a gutsy performance in Game 5?

A. Bob McClure

B. Rollie Fingers

C. Mike Caldwell

D. Pete Ladd

Answers: Singles: 1. D, 2. C, 3. B, 4. A; Doubles: 1. C, 2. B, 3. C, 4. D; Triples: 1. A, 2. B, 3. A, 4. D; Home Runs: 1. C, 2. D, 3. B, 4. A; Playoffs/World Series: 1. B, 2. A, 3. D, 4. C

New York Mets

Singles

1. Which Mets masher slugged a single-season team record 53 home runs in 2019 on his way to being named NL Rookie of the Year?

A. Michael Conforto

B. J.D. Davis

C. Pete Alonso

D. Brandon Nimmo

2. Name the Mets pitching phenom who won the NL Rookie of the Year Award in 2014 and back-to-back NL Cy Young Awards in 2018–2019.

A. Jacob deGrom

B. Steven Matz

C. Zack Wheeler

D. Noah Syndergaard

3. Which Mets all-star led the team with 29 homers and 103 RBI in 2010?

A. Carlos Delgado

B. Shawn Green

C. Carlos Beltrán

D. David Wright

4. Which Mets hero hit a dramatic and emotional eighth inning home run against the Atlanta Braves in the first MLB game played in New York City after the 9/11 tragedy?

A. Edgardo Alfonzo

B. Mike Piazza

C. Todd Zeile

D. Rey Ordóñez

Doubles

1. In what year did the New York Mets debut in their first MLB game?

A. 1960

B. 1961

C. 1963

D. 1962

2. Which Mets reliever led the NL in saves in both 1990 and 1994?

A. Armando Benítez

B. Randy Myers

C. John Franco

D. Turk Wendell

3. Which Mets all-star took home NL Rookie of the Year honors in 1983?

A. Dave Magadan

B. Darryl Strawberry

C. Gregg Jefferies

D. Hubie Brooks

4. Name the legendary Mets ace who won the NL Rookie of the Year Award in 1984 and the NL Cy Young Award in 1985, *and* captured the pitching Triple Crown in 1985.

A. Dwight Gooden

B. Ron Darling

C. Sid Fernandez

D. Roger McDowell

//

Triples

1. Which Mets slugger led the NL with 38 homers and 117 RBI in 1991?

A. Keith Hernandez

B. Howard Johnson

C. Wally Backman

D. Kevin McReynolds

2. Which Mets pitcher struck out 19 Philadelphia Phillies on the final day of the 1991 season?

A. Ron Darling

B. Roger McDowell

C. Sidd Finch

D. David Cone

3. Name the Mets player who led the NL in 1982 with 37 home runs.

A. Dave Kingman

B. Gary Carter

C. George Foster

D. Hubie Brooks

4. Which Hall of Fame Mets ace won the NL Rookie of the Year Award in 1967 and three NL Cy Young Awards in 1969, 1973, and 1975?

A. Gary Gentry

B. Tug McGraw

C. Tom Seaver

D. Nolan Ryan

Home Runs

1. Which Mets hurler led the team in 1968 with 19 victories?

A. Don Cardwell

B. Jerry Koosman

C. Jim McAndrew

D. Dick Selma

2. Which Mets pitcher tossed his way to a NL Rookie of the Year Award in 1972?

A. Jon Matlack

B. George Stone

C. Skip Lockwood

D. Bob Apodaca

3. Who was the first manager in New York Mets history?

A. Yogi Berra

B. Gil Hodges

C. Casey Stengel

D. Wes Westrum

4. Which player had the first hit in Mets history?

A. Richie Ashburn

B. Don Zimmer

C. Hobie Landrith

D. Gus Bell

Playoffs / World Series

1. Which Mets sparkplug popped a walk-off home run in Game 3 of the 1986 NLCS?

A. Mookie Wilson

B. Tim Teufel

C. Kevin Mitchell

D. Lenny Dykstra

2. Which Mets pitcher was on the mound for the final out of the incredible 1986 World Series against the Boston Red Sox?

A. Roger McDowell

B. Jesse Orosco

C. Rick Aguilera

D. Doug Sisk

3. Which three Mets players had consecutive singles in the 10th inning of Game 6 of the 1986 World Series?

A. Gary Carter, Kevin Mitchell, Ray Knight

B. Gary Carter, Kevin Mitchell, Mookie Wilson

C. Gary Carter, Ray Knight, Mookie Wilson

D. Darryl Strawberry, Ray Knight, Lenny Dykstra

4. Which Mets player earned MVP honors for his terrific performance in the 1969 World Series?

A. Ron Swoboda

B. Tommie Agee

C. Donn Clendenon

D. Cleon Jones

Mr. Met, the team's lovable official mascot, first appeared as a cartoon drawing in 1963 and then as a costumed character in 1964.

Answers: Singles: 1. C, 2. A, 3. D, 4. B; Doubles: 1. D, 2. C, 3. B, 4. A; Triples: 1. B, 2. D, 3. A, 4. C; Home Runs: 1. B, 2. A, 3. C, 4. D; Playoffs/World Series: 1. D, 2. B, 3. A, 4. C

Philadelphia Phillies

Singles

1. Which Phillies slugger mashed his way to an NL MVP Award in 2021?

A. J. T. Realmuto

B. Alec Bohm

C. Bryce Harper

D. Brandon Marsh

2. Name the Philadelphia hurler who led the staff with 17 victories in 2018.

A. Zack Wheeler

B. Taijuan Walker

C. Zach Eflin

D. Aaron Nola

3. Which Phillies thumper led the NL with 46 home runs in 2022?

A. Kyle Schwarber

B. Rhys Hoskins

C. Nick Castellanos

D. J. T. Realmuto

4. Which Philadelphia ace tossed a perfect game against the Marlins on May 29, 2010?

A. Jamie Moyer

B. Roy Halladay

C. Cole Hamels

D. Kyle Kendrick

Doubles

1. Which Phils player led the NL in hit-by-pitch three consecutive seasons from 2007–2009?

A. Shane Victorino

B. Jayson Werth

C. Plácido Polanco

D. Chase Utley

2. Which Phillies all-star led the NL in runs scored and triples in 2007, a season in which he also took home the MVP Award?

A. Carlos Ruiz

B. Shane Victorino

C. Jimmy Rollins

D. Pat Burrell

3. Which player was the Phillies' first pick in the 2002 MLB June Amateur Draft?

A. J. A. Happ

B. Cole Hamels

C. Gavin Floyd

D. Brett Myers

4. Which Phillies great snagged the NL Rookie of the Year Award in 2005 and followed it up with a NL MVP trophy in 2006?

A. Ryan Howard

B. Pat Burrell

C. Shane Victorino

D. Bobby Abreu

Triples

1. How many career home runs, Gold Gloves, and NL MVP awards did Phillies Hall of Famer Mike Schmidt record during his 18 MLB seasons?

A. 546 home runs, 10 Gold Gloves, and two NL MVPs

B. 548 home runs, 11 Gold Gloves, and three NL MVPs

C. 548 home runs, 10 Gold Gloves, and three NL MVPs

D. 558 home runs, 10 Gold Gloves, and four NL MVPs

2. Which Phillies pitching phenom led the NL in wins four consecutive seasons from 1952–1955?

A. Jim Konstanty

B. Harvey Haddix

C. Robin Roberts

D. Curt Simmons

3. Name the Phillies star who earned NL Rookie of the Year honors in 1964.

A. Johnny Callison

B. Cookie Rojas

C. Ray Culp

D. Dick Allen

4. Philadelphia's ace of aces Steve Carlton won the pitching Triple Crown in 1972 and earned the first of his four NL Cy Young Awards. How many wins did he have that season and what were his ERA and strikeout totals?

A. 26 wins, 1.98 ERA, 312 strikeouts

B. 27 wins, 1.97 ERA, 310 strikeouts

C. 25 wins, 1.99 ERA, 311 strikeouts

D. 27 wins, 1.96 ERA, 313 strikeouts

Home Runs

1. Which phantastic Phillies player won the NL batting title in both 1955 and 1958?

A. Richie Ashburn

B. Del Ennis

C. Wally Post

D. Wes Covington

2. Hall of Fame hurler Jim Bunning pitched a perfect game for the Phillies against the Mets in 1964. On which holiday did he accomplish this dazzling feat?

A. Mother's Day

B. Father's Day

C. Memorial Day

D. Independence Day

3. Which Phillies pitcher led the NL in wins four consecutive seasons, from 1914–1917?

A. Kid Gleason

B. John Coleman

C. Gus Weyhing

D. Grover Alexander

4. Name the Phillies player who batted over .400 in three different seasons (1894–1895 and 1899).

A. Sam Thompson

B. Billy Hamilton

C. Lefty O'Doul

D. Ed Delahanty

Playoffs / World Series

1. Which Phillies pitcher recorded the final out of the 2008 World Series by fanning pinch hitter Eric Hinske of the Tampa Bay Rays?

A. J. C. Romero

B. Ryan Madson

C. Brad Lidge

D. Chad Durbin

2. In Game 1 of the 1993 NLCS, which Phils hero delivered a walk-off hit in the 10th inning against the heavily favored Atlanta Braves?

A. Kim Batiste

B. Mariano Duncan

C. Wes Chamberlain

D. Kevin Stocker

3. Which Philadelphia pitcher picked up a win and two saves in the 1980 World Series, helping the Phils capture their first-ever championship title?

A. Tug McGraw

B. Dickie Noles

C. Bob Walk

D. Ron Reed

4. What was the nickname given to the 1950 Phillies, the team that won a NL pennant for the City of Brotherly Love?

A. The Fightin' Phils

B. The Whiz Kids

C. The Wonder Kids

D. The Philly Phenoms

The Philadelphia Phillies' famous mascot, the Phillie Phanatic, first debuted in 1978. His mother, the lovely Phoebe Phanatic, sometimes appears on the field alongside him.

Answers: Singles: 1. C, 2. D, 3. A, 4. B; Doubles: 1. D, 2. C, 3. B, 4. A; Triples: 1. C, 2. C, 3. D, 4. B; Home Runs: 1. A, 2. B, 3. D, 4. D; Playoffs/World Series: 1. C, 2. A, 3. A, 4. B

Singles

1. Which Pirates reliever led the NL with 39 saves in 2023?

A. Dauri Moreta

B. David Bednar

C. Colin Holderman

D. José Hernández

2. Which Pittsburgh player led the team with 37 homers and 116 RBI in 2019?

A. Josh Bell

B. Bryan Reynolds

C. Ke'Bryan Hayes

D. Starling Marte

3. Which great Bucs player earned a NL MVP Award in 2013?

A. Neil Walker

B. Garrett Jones

C. Andrew McCutchen

D. Pedro Álvarez

4. Name the Pirates player who took home the NL Rookie of the Year Award in 2004.

A. Jason Kendall

B. Jack Wilson

C. Craig Wilson

D. Jason Bay

Doubles

1. Which Pirates all-star hit his way to two NL MVP Awards in 1990 and 1992?

A. Jeff King

B. Andy Van Slyke

C. Barry Bonds

D. Sid Bream

2. The Pittsburgh Pirates traded pitcher Jose DeLeon to the Chicago White Sox for which future all-star?

A. Johnny Ray

B. Bobby Bonilla

C. Tony Peña

D. Jim Morrison

3. Which Bucs pitcher led the NL with 22 victories on his way to winning the Cy Young Award in 1990?

A. John Smiley

B. Neal Heaton

C. Bob Walk

D. Doug Drabek

4. Which Pirates powerhouse plundered his way to the NL MVP Award in 1978?

A. Dave Parker

B. Omar Moreno

C. Willie Stargell

D. Phil Garner

Triples

1. **What did Pirates legend and MLB Hall of Famer Roberto Clemente accomplish in his final regular season at-bat?**
A. He set the Pirates' single-season team record for doubles
B. He homered over the left field wall
C. He set the MLB record for most career doubles
D. He recorded his 3,000th career hit

2. **Which Bucs bomber took home the NL MVP Award in 1979?**
A. Al Oliver
B. Richie Hebner
C. Willie Stargell
D. Bob Robertson

3. **Which Pittsburgh hurler won the NL ERA title in 1955 and led the NL with 22 wins in 1958?**
A. Bob Friend
B. Harvey Haddix
C. Ron Kline
D. Vern Law

4. Which Pirates all-timer led the NL in home runs an astounding seven consecutive seasons, from 1946–1952?

A. Dick Groat

B. Ralph Kiner

C. Johnny Hopp

D. Dale Long

Home Runs

1. How many career hits did famed Pirates legend Honus Wagner tally during his 21 seasons in the big leagues?

A. 3,420

B. 3,430

C. 3,441

D. 3,450

2. Which Pirates Hall of Fame player posted a lofty .366 batting average in 1930?

A. Jake Stenzel

B. Elmer Smith

C. Kiki Cuyler

D. Pie Traynor

3. Which Pirates Hall of Famer nabbed the NL MVP Award in 1927?

A. Lloyd Waner

B. Paul Waner

C. Adam Comorosky

D. Kiki Cuyler

4. Hall of Fame infielder Arky Vaughan set the Pirates' single-season team record for batting average in 1935. What was the average he posted during that wondrous campaign?

A. .380

B. .382

C. .385

D. .402

Playoffs / World Series

1. Which Bucs reliever recorded three saves against the Baltimore Orioles in the 1979 World Series?

A. Enrique Romo

B. Kent Tekulve

C. Don Robinson

D. Grant Jackson

2. Which Pirates hero of heroes hit a walk-off home run in Game 7 of the 1960 World Series?

A. Dick Stuart

B. Don Hoak

C. Bill Mazeroski

D. Bill Virdon

3. Which Pittsburgh pitcher tossed a complete game victory in Game 7 of the 1971 World Series?

A. Steve Blass

B. Nelson Briles

C. Bob Moose

D. Dock Ellis

4. Which Pirates hurler recorded a complete game shutout in Game 7 of the 1909 World Series, giving the Bucs their first-ever title flag?

A. Vic Willis

B. Nick Maddox

C. Lefty Leifield

D. Babe Adams

The current Pittsburgh franchise formed in 1882 as Allegheny/Allegheny City, adopting the name "Pirates" unofficially in 1891 (although some sources list it as 1895).

Answers: Singles: 1. B, 2. A, 3. C, 4. D; Doubles: 1. C, 2. B, 3. D, 4. A; Triples: 1. D, 2. C, 3. A, 4. B; Home Runs: 1. A, 2. D, 3. B, 4. C; Playoffs/World Series: 1. B, 2. C, 3. A, 4. D

SAN DIEGO PADRES

Singles

1. Which exciting Padres player led the NL with 42 homers in 2021?

A. Nelson Cruz

B. Juan Soto

C. Jurickson Profar

D. Fernando Tatis Jr.

2. Name the San Diego all-star who led his squad with 32 homers and 102 RBI in 2022.

A. Juan Soto

B. Xander Bogaerts

C. Ha-Seong Kim

D. Manny Machado

3. Which Padres hurler bulled his way to a pitching Triple Crown and NL Cy Young Award in 2007?

A. Jake Peavy

B. Greg Maddux

C. Chris Young

D. David Wells

4. How many career saves did San Diego legend and Hall of Fame reliever Trevor Hoffman record during his 18 seasons on the mound?

A. 501

B. 555

C. 601

D. 701

Doubles

1. In what year did the San Diego Padres debut in their first MLB game?

A. 1968

B. 1969

C. 1970

D. 1971

2. Which Padres player had a monster season in 1996, earning himself the NL MVP Award?

A. Ken Caminiti

B. Joey Hamilton

C. Wally Joyner

D. Steve Finley

3. How many NL batting titles did the great Tony Gwynn collect during his 20 seasons in a Padres uniform?

A. 7

B. 8

C. 9

D. 10

4. Which future Hall of Famer did the San Diego Padres select in the first round of the 1973 MLB June Amateur Draft?

A. Mike Caldwell

B. Doug DeCinces

C. Ozzie Smith

D. Dave Winfield

Triples

1. Name the Padres youngster who gloved the NL Rookie of the Year Award in 1987.

A. Roberto Alomar

B. Sandy Alomar

C. Benito Santiago

D. John Kruk

2. Which San Diego pitcher led the NL with 10 complete games in 1989?

A. Ed Whitson

B. Dennis Rasmussen

C. Walt Terrell

D. Bruce Hurst

3. Bruce Bochy is the winningest manager in Padres history with 951 wins. Which skipper is second on that list with 649 victories?

A. John McNamara

B. Dick Williams

C. Bud Black

D. Roger Craig

4. Which Padres all-star hurler captured the NL Cy Young Award in 1989?

A. Mark Davis

B. Andy Hawkins

C. Jimmy Jones

D. Lance McCullers

Home Runs

1. Which player recorded the first hit—a home run—in Padres history?

A. Ed Spiezio

B. Rafael Robles

C. Roberto Peña

D. Ollie Brown

2. Which Padres all-star led his squad in homers and RBI in both 1982 and 1983?

A. Kurt Bevacqua

B. Terry Kennedy

C. Garry Templeton

D. Ruppert Jones

3. Name the San Diego pitcher who led the NL with 22 wins in 1976, earning himself the NL Cy Young Award that season.

A. Brent Strom

B. Dave Freisleben

C. Randy Jones

D. Butch Metzger

4. Which speedster holds the Padres' single-season team record for stolen bases, with 70 bags swiped in a flash?

A. Gene Richards

B. Dave Roberts

C. Alan Wiggins

D. Bip Roberts

Playoffs / World Series

1. Which Padres pitcher nabbed two victories and the MVP Award in the 1998 NLCS?

A. Joey Hamilton

B. Kevin Brown

C. Andy Ashby

D. Sterling Hitchcock

2. Which San Diego star hit a walk-off home run in Game 4 of the 1984 NLCS?

A. Steve Garvey

B. Graig Nettles

C. Carmelo Martínez

D. Kevin McReynolds

3. Name the Padres pitcher who tossed two shutout innings and earned the series-clinching win in Game 5 of the 1984 NLCS.

A. Greg Harris

B. Craig Lefferts

C. Dave Dravecky

D. Rich "Goose" Gossage

4. Which San Diego hurler took home the victory in Game 2 of the 1984 World Series?

A. Tim Lollar

B. Andy Hawkins

C. Mark Thurmond

D. Ed Whitson

The San Diego Padres were once owned by Ray Kroc, who also previously owned McDonald's.

Answers: Singles: 1. D, 2. D, 3. A, 4. C; Doubles: 1. B, 2. A, 3. B, 4. D; Triples: 1. C, 2. D, 3. C, 4. A; Home Runs: 1. A, 2. B, 3. C, 4. C; Playoffs/World Series: 1. D, 2. A, 3. B, 4. B

SAN FRANCISCO GIANTS

Singles

1. Which Giants all-star landed both the NL Rookie of the Year Award in 2010 and the NL MVP trophy in 2012?

A. Buster Posey

B. Brandon Belt

C. Brandon Crawford

D. Hunter Pence

2. Which San Francisco pitcher captured back-to-back NL Cy Young Awards in 2008–2009?

A. Matt Cain

B. Madison Bumgarner

C. Tim Lincecum

D. Ryan Vogelsong

3. Name the Giants slugger whose offensive thump landed him a NL MVP Award in 2000.

A. J. T. Snow

B. Jeff Kent

C. Rich Aurilia

D. Barry Bonds

4. For which three offensive categories does legendary San Francisco slugger Barry Bonds hold the all-time MLB career records?

A. Most career home runs, runs scored, and base on balls/walks

B. Most career home runs, base on balls/walks, and highest slugging percentage

C. Most career home runs, base on balls/walks, and highest on-base percentage

D. Most career home runs, base on balls/walks, and intentional base on balls/intentional walks

Doubles

1. Which Giants player led the NL with 109 RBI in 1988?

A. Brett Butler

B. Candy Maldonado

C. Will Clark

D. José Uribe

2. Name the San Francisco player whose monster season earned him the NL MVP Award in 1989.

A. Jeffrey Leonard

B. Kevin Mitchell

C. Ernie Riles

D. Chili Davis

3. Which Giants boomer bombed 43 home runs in 1994 to lead the NL in that strike-shortened campaign?

A. Darryl Strawberry

B. Robby Thompson

C. Deion Sanders

D. Matt Williams

4. Which San Francisco hurler had a breakout season in 1975, capturing the NL Rookie of the Year Award?

A. John Montefusco

B. Jim Barr

C. Ron Bryant

D. Pete Falcone

//

Triples

1. Which Giants slugger led the squad with 33 homers and 102 RBI in 1971?

A. Garry Maddox

B. Bobby Bonds

C. Dave Kingman

D. Gary Matthews

2. Name the San Francisco Hall of Famer who was the NL Rookie of the Year in 1959 and NL MVP in 1969.

A. Felipe Alou

B. Matty Alou

C. Willie McCovey

D. Orlando Cepeda

3. How many career wins did Giants Hall of Fame pitcher Juan Marichal record during his 16 seasons in the big leagues?

A. 243

B. 253

C. 256

D. 258

4. What number did MLB immortal Willie Mays first wear when he debuted with the New York Giants in 1951?

A. 24

B. 59

C. 38

D. 14

Home Runs

1. How many career home runs did New York Giants Hall of Famer Mel Ott hit during his 22 seasons at the old Polo Grounds?

A. 511

B. 512

C. 513

D. 515

2. How many World Series titles and NL pennants did legendary New York Giants manager John McGraw collect during his 30-plus years as a skipper?

A. 2 World Series titles and 7 NL pennants

B. 3 World Series titles and 8 NL pennants

C. 3 World Series titles and 9 NL pennants

D. 3 World Series titles and 10 NL pennants

3. Which pitcher holds the Giants' single-season team record for wins with 44 victories way back in 1885?

A. Amos Rusie

B. Tim Keefe

C. Mickey Welch

D. Joe McGinnity

4. Which ill-fated Brooklyn Dodgers pitcher gave up the famed "Shot Heard 'Round the World" home run to New York Giants hero Bobby Thomson, which clinched the NL pennant for the Giants in 1951?

A. Clem Labine

B. Ralph Branca

C. Don Newcombe

D. Clyde King

Playoffs / World Series

1. Which San Francisco favorite cracked three home runs in Game 1 of the 2012 World Series?

A. Ángel Pagán

B. Brandon Belt

C. Marco Scutaro

D. Pablo Sandoval

2. Which Cleveland batter hit the ball that Giants centerfielder Willie Mays famously caught over his shoulder in the eighth inning of Game 1 of the 1954 World Series?

A. Al Smith

B. Larry Doby

C. Vic Wertz

D. Bobby Ávila

3. In Game 4 of the 1933 World Series, which New York Giants ace pitched 11 innings to secure a 2–1 victory against the Washington Senators/Nationals?

A. Freddie Fitzsimmons

B. Carl Hubbell

C. Roy Parmelee

D. Hal Schumacher

4. Which New York pitching wizard recorded three complete game shutouts against the Philadelphia Athletics in the 1905 World Series to clinch the first-ever MLB championship for the Giants?

A. Christy Mathewson

B. Red Ames

C. Hooks Wiltse

D. Rube Marquard

Giants Hall of Famer Bill Terry is the last NL player to bat over .400, posting a .401 mark in 1930.

SAN FRANCISCO GIANTS

Answers: Singles: 1. A, 2. C, 3. B, 4. D; Doubles: 1. C, 2. B, 3. D, 4. A; Triples: 1. B, 2. C, 3. A, 4. D; Home Runs: 1. A, 2. D, 3. C, 4. B; Playoffs/World Series: 1. D, 2. C, 3. B, 4. A

189

St. Louis Cardinals

Singles

1. Which Cardinals clubber came away with the NL MVP Award in 2022?

A. Tyler O'Neill
B. Paul Goldschmidt
C. Nolan Arenado
D. Lars Nootbaar

2. How many wins did St. Louis pitcher Adam Wainwright record in his 18-year career with the Redbirds?

A. 198
B. 199
C. 200
D. 201

3. Which Cardinals all-timer tallied nine Gold Glove and four Platinum Glove awards from 2008–2018?

A. Matt Holliday
B. Skip Schumaker
C. Jon Jay
D. Yadier Molina

4. Which St. Louis player earned the NL Rookie of the Year crown in 2001 and then three NL MVP Awards in 2005, 2008, and 2009?

A. Scott Rolen
B. Jim Edmonds
C. Albert Pujols
D. Ryan Ludwick

Doubles

1. How many career Gold Glove Awards did Cardinals shortstop Ozzie Smith, "the Wizard," collect during his 19 seasons in the big leagues?

A. 13
B. 14
C. 15
D. 16

2. Which St. Louis all-star won the NL MVP Award in 1985?

A. Tom Herr
B. Willie McGee
C. Terry Pendleton
D. Lonnie Smith

3. Name the Cardinals Hall of Fame reliever who led the NL in saves in 1981, 1982, and 1984.

A. Ricky Horton

B. Neil Allen

C. Bruce Sutter

D. Lee Smith

4. Which slick-fielding Cardinals player won the NL batting title and MVP Award in 1979?

A. Keith Hernandez

B. George Hendrick

C. Tony Scott

D. Ted Simmons

//

Triples

1. How many stolen bases did Cardinals great Lou Brock record during his 19-year Hall of Fame career?

A. 928

B. 933

C. 935

D. 938

2. Cardinals Hall of Fame pitcher Bob Gibson won both the NL Cy Young and MVP Awards in 1968. What was his ERA during that season?

A. 1.07

B. 1.08

C. 1.12

D. 1.14

3. How many NL MVP Awards and NL batting titles did St. Louis icon Stan "the Man" Musial record in his 22-year Hall of Fame career?

A. Three NL MVP Awards and five NL batting titles

B. Four NL MVP Awards and six NL batting titles

C. Four NL MVP Awards and seven NL batting titles

D. Three NL MVP Awards and seven NL batting titles

4. Which Cardinals Hall of Famer led the NL in 1939 with a .349 batting average?

A. Jimmy Brown

B. Johnny Mize

C. Pepper Martin

D. Enos Slaughter

Home Runs

1. What was the career batting average of Cardinals king of swing Rogers Hornsby, perhaps the greatest hitter in St. Louis and MLB history?

A. .356

B. .357

C. .358

D. .359

2. Which Cardinals pitcher tallied 30 wins in 1934 to nab the NL MVP Award that season?

A. Dizzy Dean

B. Paul "Daffy" Dean

C. Dazzy Vance

D. Tex Carleton

3. Which St. Louis superstar took home the NL MVP award in 1937, a season in which he hit for the Triple Crown?

A. Pepper Martin

B. Joe Medwick

C. Leo Durocher

D. Frankie Frisch

4. Which pitcher holds the St. Louis franchise single-season team record for wins with 45 (yes, 45!) victories back in the summer of 1888?

A. Silver King

B. Dave Foutz

C. Bob Caruthers

D. Ice Box Chamberlain

Playoffs / World Series

1. Which Cardinals cult hero hit a walk-off home run in the 11th inning of Game 6 of the 2011 World Series?

A. Nick Punto

B. David Freese

C. Lance Berkman

D. Allen Craig

2. Name the St. Louis Redbird whose clutch performance earned him MVP honors in the 1982 World Series.

A. Dane Iorg

B. Ken Oberkfell

C. Darrell Porter

D. Ozzie Smith

3. In Game 7 of the 1946 World Series, which Cardinals baserunner flew home with the winning run in the eighth inning?

A. Enos Slaughter

B. Joe Garagiola

C. Red Schoendienst

D. Harry Walker

4. Which New York Yankees player was thrown out trying to steal second base to end Game 7 of the 1926 World Series, giving the Cardinals their first-ever MLB championship?

A. Bob Meusel

B. Tony Lazzeri

C. Lou Gehrig

D. Babe Ruth

Cardinals behemoth Mark McGwire belted 135 combined home runs in just two seasons (1998–1999), crushing 220 total dingers in just 545 games with St. Louis.

Singles

1. Which Nationals natural won a NL batting title in 2020?

A. Juan Soto

B. Trea Turner

C. Howie Kendrick

D. Carter Kieboom

2. Which Washington fireballer won back-to-back NL Cy Young Awards in 2016–2017?

A. Tanner Roark

B. Max Scherzer

C. Gio González

D. Joe Ross

3. Which player did Washington take as the first overall pick in the first round of the 2009 MLB June Amateur Draft?

A. Drew Storen

B. Michael A. Taylor

C. Stephen Strasburg

D. Marcus Stroman

4. Which future NL Rookie of the Year and NL MVP did the Nationals take as the first overall pick in the first round of the 2010 MLB June Amateur Draft?

A. A. J. Cole

B. Matt Grace

C. Robbie Ray

D. Bryce Harper

Doubles

1. In what year did the Montreal Expos debut in their first MLB game?

A. 1968

B. 1969

C. 1970

D. 1971

2. In what year did the Montreal Expos move to Washington and become the Nationals?

A. 2004

B. 2005

C. 2006

D. 2007

3. Which exceptional Expos player led the NL with 206 hits in 2002?

A. Andrés Galarraga

B. Orlando Cabrera

C. Vladimir Guerrero

D. Fernando Tatís

4. Which Montreal pitcher petrified batters on his way to a NL Cy Young Award in 1997?

A. Pedro Martínez

B. Jeff Juden

C. Carlos Pérez

D. Dustin Hermanson

Triples

1. Which Montreal Hall of Famer earned NL Rookie of the Year honors in 1977?

A. Larry Parrish

B. Tim Raines

C. Gary Carter

D. Andre Dawson

2. Which Expos all-star led the NL with 106 RBI in 1984?

A. Terry Francona

B. Pete Rose

C. Gary Carter

D. Jim Wohlford

3. How many stolen bases did Montreal speedster Tim Raines tally in his 23-year Hall of Fame career?

A. 805

B. 806

C. 807

D. 808

4. Which Expos standout led the NL in doubles in both 1987 and 1989?

A. Hubie Brooks

B. Tim Wallach

C. Marquis Grissom

D. Larry Walker

Home Runs

1. Which player had the first hit in Montreal Expos history?

A. Maury Wills

B. Mack Jones

C. Bob Bailey

D. Gary Sutherland

2. Which player had the first hit in modern Washington Nationals history?

A. Brad Wilkerson

B. Christian Guzman

C. José Vidro

D. Ryan Zimmerman

3. Which pitcher holds the Montreal Expos/Washington Nationals team record for most career wins, with 158 victories?

A. Steve Rogers

B. Steve Renko

C. Bill Gullickson

D. Dennis Martínez

4. Which beloved MLB player led the Expos with 29 home runs in 1969?

A. Ron Hunt

B. Tim McCarver

C. Ken Singleton

D. Rusty Staub

Washington debuted the Presidents Race in 2006. In this promotional event, held in the middle of the fourth inning of every Nationals home game, Founding Father mascots topped with giant foam heads compete in a footrace (go, Teddy, go!).

Playoffs / World Series

1. Which Nationals pitcher picked up the save in Game 1 of the 2019 World Series?

A. Sean Doolittle

B. Parick Corbin

C. Aníbal Sánchez

D. Joe Ross

2. Which Washington player belted a home run off the St. Louis Cardinals' Adam Wainwright in Game 2 of the 2019 NLCS?

A. Kurt Suzuki

B. Trea Turner

C. Adam Eaton

D. Michael A. Taylor

3. In Game 7 of the 2019 World Series, which clutch Nationals player hit a go-ahead home run in the seventh inning?

A. Yan Gomes

B. Howie Kendrick

C. Anthony Rendon

D. Asdrúbal Cabrera

4. Which Washington pitcher was on the mound for the final out of the 2019 World Series?

A. Tanner Rainey

B. Javy Guerra

C. Daniel Hudson

D. Fernando Rodney

Answers: Singles: 1. A, 2. B, 3. C, 4. D; Doubles: 1. B, 2. B, 3. C, 4. A; Triples: 1. D, 2. C, 3. D, 4. B; Home Runs: 1. C, 2. A, 3. A, 4. D; Playoffs/World Series: 1. A, 2. D, 3. B, 4. C

Extra
INNINGS

Everybody loves extra innings, so here
are some bonus trivia questions! There
are no points to score for these final
three quizzes—these are strictly for fun.

1. Which player holds the Arizona Diamondbacks' team record for most career triples with 52 three-baggers?

A. David Peralta

B. Stephen Drew

C. Ketel Marte

D. Nick Ahmed

2. How many wins did Boston/ Milwaukee Braves Hall of Fame pitcher Warren Spahn record in his 21-year career?

A. 360

B. 362

C. 363

D. 366

3. Which pitcher holds the Baltimore Orioles' single-season team record for saves, with 51 to his credit?

A. Zack Britton

B. Randy Myers

C. Gregg Olson

D. Jim Johnson

4. Which two BoSox players won the AL MVP Award in 1995 and the AL Rookie of the Year Award in 1997?

A. Mo Vaughn (MVP) and Nomar Garciaparra (Rookie of the Year)

B. John Valentin (MVP) and Troy O'Leary (Rookie of the Year)

C. Mike Greenwell (MVP) and Michael Coleman (Rookie of the Year)

D. Jose Canseco (MVP) and Jason Varitek (Rookie of the Year)

5. Which Chicago Cubs pitcher posted a 16–1 record with the club in 1984, roaring his way to a NL Cy Young Award that season?

A. Scott Sanderson

B. Steve Trout

C. Rick Sutcliffe

D. Dennis Eckersley

6. In what year did the Chicago White Sox allegedly "throw" the World Series, allowing the Cincinnati Reds to capture the title?

A. 1915

B. 1916

C. 1918

D. 1919

7. Which Cincinnati Reds pitcher is the only player in MLB history to throw two consecutive no-hitters?

A. Peaches Davis

B. Johnny Vander Meer

C. Paul Derringer

D. Bucky Walters

8. Which Cleveland all-star caught AL Rookie of the Year honors in 1990?

A. Sandy Alomar Jr.

B. Jim Thome

C. Carlos Baerga

D. Jerry Browne

9. Which team is the triple-A affiliate of the Colorado Rockies?

A. Hartford Yard Goats

B. Albuquerque Isotopes

C. El Paso Chihuahuas

D. Round Rock Express

10. Which pitcher holds the Detroit Tigers' career team record for saves, with a total of 235?

A. Willie Hernández

B. Aurelio López

C. Todd Jones

D. Mike Henneman

11. Which Houston Astros standout batted .355 with 30 homers and 114 RBI in 2000?

A. Moisés Alou

B. Richard Hidalgo

C. Jeff Bagwell

D. Lance Berkman

12. Which cool Kansas City Royals character walked away with the AL Rookie of the Year Award in 1999?

A. Jermaine Dye

B. Johnny Damon

C. Mike Sweeney

D. Carlos Beltrán

13. In what year did the Los Angeles Angels debut in their first MLB game?

A. 1958

B. 1959

C. 1960

D. 1961

14. Which Brooklyn Dodgers ace won the NL pitching triple crown in 1924, earning himself the MVP Award that season?

A. Burleigh Grimes

B. Dazzy Vance

C. Dutch Ruether

D. Dutch Henry

15. Which Florida Marlins pitcher recorded the first victory in franchise history?

A. Al Leiter

B. Jack Armstrong

C. Charlie Hough

D. Chris Hammond

16. Which Milwaukee Brewers all-star pitcher earned both the AL Cy Young and MVP Awards in 1981?

A. Rollie Fingers

B. Bob McClure

C. Reggie Cleveland

D. Moose Haas

17. Which Herculean Minnesota Twins hurler tossed 10 shutout innings in Game 7 of the 1991 World Series?

A. Rick Aguilera

B. Jack Morris

C. Kevin Tapani

D. Scott Erickson

18. Name the player who holds the New York Mets' single-season team record for hits, with 227 base knocks.

A. John Olerud

B. Keith Hernandez

C. José Reyes

D. Lance Johnson

19. In the eighth inning of Game 1 of the 1996 ALCS, which spectator leaned over the wall in right field and turned a Derek Jeter fly ball into a home run?

A. Jim Myers

B. Jeffrey Madison

C. Jeffrey Maier

D. John Mayor

20. Which Oakland A's thumper snagged the AL MVP Award in 2000?

A. Miguel Tejada

B. Olmedo Sáenz

C. Jason Giambi

D. Jeremy Giambi

21. Which fine Philadelphia Phillies phenom nabbed a NL Rookie of the Year Award in 1997?

A. Scott Rolen

B. Mike Lieberthal

C. Kevin Jordan

D. Ricky Bottalico

22. Which Pittsburgh Pirates pitcher won the NL ERA title in 1977 and also led the Bucs with 20 wins that year?

A. Bruce Kison

B. Jerry Reuss

C. Jim Rooker

D. John Candelaria

23. What is the name of the famed San Diego Padres team mascot who first appeared in 1974?

A. The San Diego Sand Shark

B. The San Diego Chicken

C. The San Diego Singing Sensation

D. S. D. "Special Delivery" Jones

24. In what year did the New York Giants move to San Francisco?

A. 1955

B. 1956

C. 1957

D. 1958

25. Who was the famed lead play-by-play announcer for the Seattle Mariners from 1977–2010?

A. Ernie Harwell

B. Red Barber

C. Dave Niehaus

D. Vin Scully

26. Which St. Louis Cardinals player earned 2006 World Series MVP honors for his great effort against the Detroit Tigers?

A. David Eckstein
B. Chris Carpenter
C. Ronnie Belliard
D. Braden Looper

27. Which slugger led the Tampa Bay Devil Rays with 34 homers and 107 RBI in 2003?

A. Travis Lee
B. Aubrey Huff
C. Carlos Peña
D. Rocco Baldelli

28. Name the Texas Rangers pitcher who led the AL with 277 strikeouts in 2013.

A. Matt Harrison
B. Scott Feldman
C. Yu Darvish
D. Derek Holland

29. Which Toronto Blue Jays bopper was named MVP of the 1992 ALCS?

A. Joe Carter
B. Kelly Gruber
C. Manuel Lee
D. Roberto Alomar

30. Who was both the last manager of the Montreal Expos and the first manager of the modern Washington Nationals?

A. Manny Acta
B. Jim Riggleman
C. Davey Johnson
D. Frank Robinson

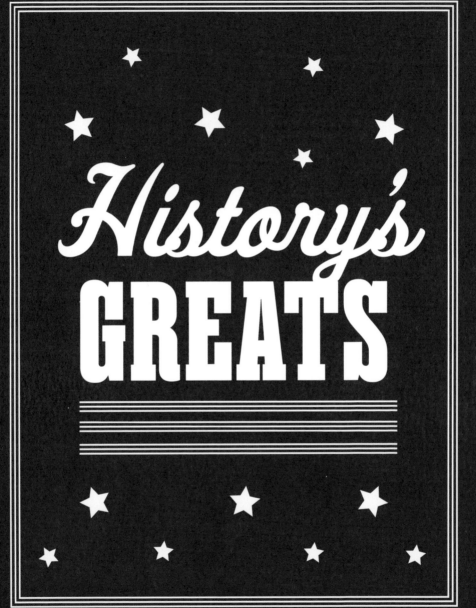

History's
GREATS

1. How old was future Hall of Fame pitcher Satchel Paige when he tossed three shutout innings against the Boston Red Sox in 1965?

A. 57

B. 58

C. 59

D. 60

2. Which team did Hall of Fame slugger Josh Gibson first debut with in 1930?

A. The Pittsburgh Crawfords

B. The Memphis Red Sox

C. The Kansas City Monarchs

D. The Homestead Grays

3. Which St. Louis Stars Hall of Fame player collected a whopping 33 doubles in 1925?

A. Dewey Creacy

B. Candy Jim Taylor

C. Willie Wells

D. Cool Papa Bell

4. Name the Homestead Grays Hall of Fame slugger who posted a lofty .420 BA in 1938.

A. Buck Leonard

B. Sam Bankhead

C. Jelly Jackson

D. Vic Harris

5. Which team did Hall of Fame legend Hank Aaron first sign with before inking a deal with the Boston Braves?

A. The Birmingham Black Barons

B. The Indianapolis Clowns

C. The Cleveland Cubs

D. The Cleveland Buckeyes

6. What does AAGPBL stand for regarding women's professional baseball?

A. All-Atlantic Girls Professional Baseball League

B. All-Athletic Girls Professional Baseball League

C. American-Association Girls Professional Baseball League

D. All-American Girls Professional Baseball League

7. In what year did the AAGPBL teams play in their first games?

A. 1941

B. 1942

C. 1943

D. 1944

8. Where were initial tryouts held for potential AAGPBL players?

A. Yankee Stadium

B. Fenway Park

C. Wrigley Field

D. The Polo Grounds

9. Which AAGPBL team won four championship titles, the most of any squad?

A. The Milwaukee Chicks

B. The Rockford Peaches

C. The Racine Belles

D. The South Bend Blue Sox

10. What popular 1992 film was based on the wonderful history of the AAGPBL?

A. *A League of Their Own*

B. *A League for the Ladies*

C. *The Gallant Gals of Baseball*

D. *Darlings of the Diamond*

11. Which AAGPBL team took home the first-ever league championship in 1943?

A. Milwaukee Chicks

B. Rockford Peaches

C. Racine Belles

D. Grand Rapids Chicks

12. Which AAGPBL team took home the last league championship in 1954?

A. South Bend Blue Sox

B. Kalamazoo Lassies

C. Kenosha Comets

D. Fort Wayne Daisies

13. Which star won the first-ever AAGPBL Player of the Year Award in 1945?

A. Connie Wisniewski

B. Betty Foss

C. Audrey Wagner

D. Sophie Kurys

14. Which two stars won the AAGPBL Player of the Year Award twice?

A. Audrey Wagner and Alma Ziegler

B. Connie Wisniewski and Sophie Kurys

C. Betty Foss and Joanne Weaver

D. Doris Sams and Jean Faut

15. In what year was the AAGPBL officially inducted into the National Baseball Hall of Fame?

A. 1986

B. 1987

C. 1988

D. 1989

16. Who was the first Black player in the history of both the St. Louis Browns and New York Giants?

A. Dan Bankhead

B. Hank Thompson

C. Ray Noble

D. Artie Wilson

17. Which player is considered by some historians to be the first-ever Black player in MLB history, making his debut in 1884?

A. Moses Fleetwood Walker

B. Dave Pope

C. Quincy Trouppe

D. Bob Trice

18. Which Hall of Fame St. Louis Stars player won the Negro National League (NNL) batting Triple Crown in 1930?

A. Branch Russell

B. John Henry Russell

C. Willie Wells

D. Mule Suttles

19. Which Hall of Fame superstar won back-to-back Eastern Colored League (ECL) batting Triple Crowns in 1924–1925?

A. Fats Jenkins

B. Hen Jordan

C. Pepper Daniels

D. Oscar Charleston

20. Which Hall of Fame pitching ace led the Negro National League II (NN2) in wins five times (1935, 1937, 1938, 1940, and 1942)?

A. Rube Foster

B. Ray Brown

C. Smokey Joe Williams

D. Bullet Rogan

Answers: 1. C, 2. B, 3. D, 4. A, 5. B, 6. D, 7. C, 8. C, 9. B, 10. A, 11. C, 12. B, 13. A, 14. D, 15. C, 16. B, 17. A, 18. C, 19. D, 20. B

HISTORY'S GREATS

221

Way Back
TRIVIA

1. How many career wins did nineteenth-century Hall of Fame pitching legend Old Hoss Radbourn tally in his 11 seasons on the mound?

A. 291

B. 302

C. 310

D. 314

2. Old Hoss Radbourn holds the all-time MLB record for most wins in a single season. How many victories did he earn, and in what year did he accomplish this feat?

A. 56 wins in 1880

B. 58 wins in 1882

C. 59 wins in 1883

D. 60 wins in 1884

3. Which Hall of Fame player captured four National League batting titles in 1879, 1881, 1887, and 1888?

A. Cap Anson

B. Ed Andrews

C. Sam Crane

D. Jerry Denny

4. Which Buffalo Bisons Hall of Fame standout led the National League in batting averages in both 1882 and 1883?

A. Deacon White

B. Jim O'Rourke

C. Jack Rowe

D. Dan Brouthers

5. Which Buffalo Bisons Hall of Fame pitcher notched a staggering 46 wins and 72 complete games in 1883?

A. George Derby

B. Pud Galvin

C. Ed Cushman

D. Art Hagan

6. When and where was MLB Hall of Fame legend George Herman "Babe" Ruth born?

A. 1895 in Baltimore, Maryland

B. 1896 in Boston, Massachusetts

C. 1897 in Albany, New York

D. 1898 in Newark, New Jersey

7. Which Philadelphia Phillies pitcher led his squad in 1890 with 38 victories?

A. Billy Sunday

B. Tom Vickery

C. Kid Gleason

D. Phenomenal Smith

8. Which Hall of Fame speedster stole 100 or more bases three straight seasons from 1889–1891?

A. Sam Thompson

B. Ed Delahanty

C. Billy Shindle

D. Billy Hamilton

9. Hall of Fame pitcher Cy Young debuted in 1890 with which team?

A. Louisville Colonels

B. Cleveland Spiders

C. Brooklyn Dodgers

D. Boston Americans

10. Which Hall of Fame player had an amazing 44-game hitting streak in 1897?

A. Willie Keeler

B. Home Run Baker

C. Henry Reitz

D. Hughie Jennings

11. Nineteenth-century mound ace Will White is credited with being the first major league player to do what on the baseball field?

A. Pitch a perfect game

B. Wear spikes

C. Throw a spitball

D. Wear eyeglasses

12. Which Hall of Fame player led the National Association in 1875 with a .367 batting average?

A. Davy Force

B. Lip Pike

C. Deacon White

D. Pop Snyder

13. Name the Hall of Fame pitcher who led the National League in wins three straight seasons from 1896–1898.

A. Bill Hoffer

B. Kid Nichols

C. Frank Dwyer

D. Clark Griffith

14. Which club did Hall of Fame infielder Roger Connor debut with in 1880?

A. Worcester Ruby Legs

B. Cleveland Blues

C. Providence Grays

D. Troy Trojans

15. Which Boston pitcher led the National League in wins in both 1877 and 1878, notching consecutive 40-win seasons?

A. Tommy Bond

B. Jim Devlin

C. Terry Larkin

D. The Only Nolan

16. Which pitcher led the American Association in 1885 with 40 wins and a 2.07 earned run average?

A. Jimmy Peoples

B. Bob Caruthers

C. Hank O'Day

D. Ed Knouff

17. Which Hall of Fame twirler co-led the National League with 42 victories in 1886, sharing the win title with fellow pitcher Lady Baldwin?

A. Dupee Shaw

B. Ed Morris

C. Egyptian Healy

D. Tim Keefe

18. In 1897, which Hall of Fame player led the National League with 135 RBI?

A. George Davis

B. Nap Lajoie

C. Jimmy Collins

D. Hugh Duffy

19. Which pitcher had the odd distinction of leading the National League in both wins (31) and losses (33) in 1881?

A. George Derby

B. Lee Richmond

C. Jim Whitney

D. Fred Goldsmith

20. Name the infielder who led the National League in hits in consecutive seasons from 1889–1890.

A. Dave Orr

B. Jack Glasscock

C. Tommy Tucker

D. Bug Holliday

21. Which slugger led the American Association in 1890 with a .363 batting average?

A. Spud Johnson

B. John Ward

C. Chicken Wolf

D. Hardy Richardson

22. Which Hall of Fame hurler captured the National League pitching Triple Crown in 1889?

A. John Clarkson

B. Gus Weyhing

C. Jesse Duryea

D. Matt Kilroy

23. Which Chicago White Stockings batting champ hit the first home run in National League history in 1876?

A. John Glenn

B. John Peters

C. Bob Addy

D. Ross Barnes

24. Name the Hall of Fame ace who pocketed the National League pitching Triple Crown in 1894.

A. Amos Rusie

B. Kid Carsey

C. Brickyard Kennedy

D. Adonis Terry

25. Which player led the American Association in runs scored three straight seasons from 1883–1885?

A. Charley Jones

B. Arlie Latham

C. Harry Stovey

D. Lon Knight

26. Which Hall of Fame outfielder led the National League in 1894 with a robust .440 batting average?

A. Tuck Turner

B. Hugh Duffy

C. Joe Kelley

D. Lave Cross

27. Which Cleveland Blues hurler gave batters the blues, leading the National League with 45 wins in 1880?

A. Larry Corcoran

B. Jim McCormick

C. Curry Foley

D. John Ward

28. Pete Browning of the Cleveland Infants won a batting title in 1890 with a .373 clip. When he recorded this mark, which league did he play for?

A. National Association

B. American Association

C. Players League

D. National League

29. Star pitcher Tony Mullane holds a dubious all-time MLB career record in which category?

A. Most career home runs allowed

B. Most career walks allowed

C. Most career runs allowed

D. Most career wild pitches

30. Which Hall of Fame infielder led the Players League in 1890 with 22 triples?

A. Jake Beckley

B. Jocko Fields

C. Billy Shindle

D. Bill Joyce

31. Which Boston pitcher tallied a whopping 48 victories in 1884?

A. Daisy Davis

B. Cy Young

C. Smoky Joe Wood

D. Charlie Buffinton

32. Which Hall of Fame Cleveland Spiders clubber spun his way to back-to-back National League batting titles in 1895 and 1896?

A. Cupid Childs

B. Mike Tiernan

C. Jesse Burkett

D. Elmer Smith

33. Paul Hines won the National League batting Triple Crown in 1878 starring for which squad?

A. Providence Grays

B. Milwaukee Grays

C. Cincinnati Reds

D. Indianapolis Blues

34. Which amazing Hall of Fame pitcher led all of MLB in wins six straight seasons, from 1871–1876, and also still holds the all-time MLB career record in Win-Loss Percentage with a mind-boggling .794 clip?

A. Dick McBride

B. Al Spalding

C. Jim Britt

D. George Zettlein

35. Which Hall of Fame player led the National League in homers in 1883 and triples in 1884?

A. Jack Rowe

B. Joe Hornung

C. Buck Ewing

D. Jack Burdock

36. Which St. Louis Browns superstar won the American Association batting Triple Crown in 1887?

A. Charlie Comiskey

B. Tip O'Neill

C. John Corkhill

D. Joe Werrick

37. How many career hits did Hall of Famer King Kelly record in his stellar 16 seasons in the big leagues?

A. 1,813

B. 1,947

C. 2,008

D. 2,122

38. Hall of Fame infielder Hughie Jennings holds the all-time MLB career record in which category?

A. Most career total bases

B. Most career at bats

C. Most career plate appearances

D. Most career hits-by-pitch

39. The Union Association was a league that lasted only one season (1884). Which team won the Pennant in that lone campaign?

A. Wilmington Quicksteps

B. Baltimore Monumentals

C. St. Louis Maroons

D. Cincinnati Outlaw Reds

40. In what year was the distance from the mound to home plate first set at 60 feet, 6 inches?

A. 1890

B. 1891

C. 1892

D. 1893

Answers: 1. C, 2. D, 3. A, 4. D, 5. B, 6. A, 7. C, 8. D, 9. B, 10. A, 11. D, 12. C, 13. B, 14. D, 15. A, 16. B, 17. D, 18. A, 19. C, 20. B, 21. C, 22. A, 23. D, 24. A, 25. C, 26. B, 27. B, 28. C, 29. D, 30. A, 31. D, 32. C, 33. A, 34. B, 35. C, 36. B, 37. A, 38. D, 39. C, 40. D

Last Up!

1. In what year was the first MLB All-Star Game?

A. 1931

B. 1932

C. 1933

D. 1934

2. In what venue was the first MLB All-Star Game held?

A. Shibe Park

B. Comiskey Park

C. Ebbets Field

D. Forbes Field

3. Which player holds the single-season MLB record for sacrifice flies, with 19 in a lone campaign?

A. Gil Hodges

B. Reggie Smith

C. Howard Johnson

D. Francisco Lindor

4. Which hard-hitting ballplayer won two NL batting titles with the Chicago Cubs (1975-1976) and another two NL batting titles with the Pittsburgh Pirates (1981 and 1983)?

A. Phil Garner

B. José Cardenal

C. Andre Thornton

D. Bill Madlock

LAST UP!

5. Which BoSox batter bashed his way to an AL MVP Award in 1958?

A. Pete Runnels

B. Frank Malzone

C. Jackie Jensen

D. Jimmy Piersall

6. Which Philadelphia Phillies player batted .398 with 254 hits in 1929, leading the NL in hits and winning the batting title to boot?

A. Pinky Whitney

B. Don Hurst

C. Fresco Thompson

D. Lefty O'Doul

7. Which Detroit Tigers batter mauled opposing pitchers in 1926, winning the AL batting title with a .378 mark?

A. Jack Warner

B. Heinie Manush

C. Frank O'Rourke

D. Jackie Tavener

8. In what year did legendary owner George Steinbrenner purchase the New York Yankees?

A. 1970

B. 1971

C. 1973

D. 1974

9. Which Philadelphia Phillies Hall of Famer took home NL MVP honors in 1932?

A. Ray Benge

B. Chuck Klein

C. Curt Davis

D. Cy Williams

10. In what year did the American League first introduce the designated hitter (DH) and which player was the first DH in MLB history?

A. 1973, Ron Blomberg

B. 1974, Jerry Moses

C. 1975, Carlos May

D. 1976, Lee May

11. In what year did baseball legend Jackie Robinson debut and break the MLB color barrier?

A. 1945

B. 1946

C. 1947

D. 1948

12. Pitcher Roger Clemens of the Boston Red Sox had two 20-strikeout games—one in 1986 against the Seattle Mariners and one in 1996 against the Detroit Tigers. Who were his catchers in each of those games?

A. Marc Sullivan (1986) and Bill Haselman (1996)

B. Rich Gedman (1986) and Mike Stanley (1996)

C. Rich Gedman (1986) and Bill Haselman (1996)

D. Marc Sullivan (1986) and Scott Hatteberg (1996)

POST-SEASON

MLB *Fast Facts*

Baseball is full of stats but also facts—interesting details about the game itself. Here are a few you may not have known about the sport.

- **Cincinnati Reds** pitcher **Joe Nuxhall** is the youngest player in MLB history, debuting in 1944 at the age of 15.

- **Brooklyn Dodgers** infielder **Tommy Brown** is the second youngest player in MLB history, debuting in 1944 at the age of 16.

- Hall of Fame pitcher **Cy Young** holds the MLB record for most career wins with 511 victories.

- **St. Louis Cardinals** slugger **Fernando Tatís** is the only player in MLB history to hit two grand slams in one inning. He accomplished this feat against the **Los Angeles Dodgers** on April 23, 1999.

- **Arizona Diamondbacks** pitcher **Randy Johnson** tossed a perfect game against the **Atlanta Braves** on May 18, 2004.

- **Phil Plantier** holds the MLB record for most career home runs hit by a player born in New Hampshire with 91.

- **Chicago White Sox** pitcher **Philip Humber** threw a perfect game against the **Seattle Mariners** on April 21, 2012.

- Former MLB player **Ron Hunt** led the NL in HPB (hit by pitch) seven consecutive seasons from 1968–1974.

- **Del Bissonette** holds the MLB record for most career home runs hit by a player born in Maine with 66.

- **St. Louis Cardinals** Hall of Famer **Stan Musial** had 3,630 career hits—with exactly 1,815 at home and 1,815 on the road.

- The official mascot of the **Colorado Rockies** is a purple Triceratops named Dinger.

- Billy the Marlin is the official mascot of the **Miami Marlins**. He is listed as being eight feet tall.

- **San Diego Padres** pitcher **Eric Show** surrendered **Pete Rose's** record-breaking 4,192nd career hit on September 11, 1985.

- **Sadaharu Oh** holds the world career home run record with 868 tater tots, playing with the **Yomiuri Giants** from 1959–1980.

- **Masanori Murakami** is the first Japanese-born player in MLB history, debuting with the **San Francisco Giants** in 1964.

- Little League Baseball was founded in Williamsport, Pennsylvania, in 1939. The Little League World Series is held annually every August in South Williamsport, Pennsylvania.

- The College World Series is held annually every June in Omaha, Nebraska.

- The Major League Baseball logo was designed by Jerry Dior in 1968.

- A standard MLB baseball has 108 double-sided stitches—or 216 if you count the hidden stitches on the seams.

- Before being used in a game, all MLB baseballs are rubbed up with **Lena Blackburne** Baseball Rubbing Mud taken from the New Jersey side of the Delaware River.

- Baseball historians generally agree that the first all-professional baseball team was the **Cincinnati Red Stockings** of 1869.

- Hall of Fame pitcher **Randy Johnson** won four consecutive NL Cy Young Awards with the **Arizona Diamondbacks** from 1999–2002.

- **Baltimore Orioles** slugger **Eddie Murray** led the AL with 22 home runs during the strike-shortened season of 1981.

- Hall of Fame Boston icon **Carl Yastrzemski** claimed the AL MVP Award in 1967 and also won the Triple Crown in that remarkable season.

- Boston's **Fenway Park** is the oldest active ballpark in MLB, first opening its gates in 1912.

- **Cincinnati Reds** pitcher **Tom Browning** threw a perfect game against the **Los Angeles Dodgers** on September 16, 1988.

- **The Kansas City Royals** debuted in their first MLB game in 1969.

- **Lou Piniella** had the first hit in **Kansas City Royals** history, winning the AL Rookie of the Year Award in 1969.

- **Los Angeles Dodgers** superhuman pitching great **Sandy Koufax** threw a perfect game against the **Chicago Cubs** on September 9, 1965.

- **Los Angeles Dodgers** reliever **Eric Gagné** converted an MLB-record 84 consecutive saves from 2002–2004 and also captured the 2003 NL Cy Young Award.

- **New York Yankees** pitchers have thrown four perfect games, an MLB record: **Don Larsen** in 1956 (World Series), **David Wells** in 1998, **David Cone** in 1999, and **Domingo Germán** in 2023.

- **Cornelius McGillicuddy**, better known as **Connie Mack**, both owned and managed the **Philadelphia Athletics** for their first 50 seasons (1901–1950).

- **Oakland A's** pitcher **Dallas Braden** threw a perfect game against the **Tampa Bay Rays** on May 9, 2010.

- **Philadelphia Phillies** reliever **Steve Bedrosian** led the NL with 40 saves in 1987, winning both the Cy Young Award and Rolaids Relief Man of the Year title that season.

- **Philadelphia Phillies** Hall of Famer **Mike Schmidt** cracked four homers in a single game against the **Chicago Cubs** on April 17, 1976.

- **Pittsburgh Pirates** Hall of Fame brothers **Paul** and **Lloyd Waner** were known as "Big Poison" and "Little Poison," and both starred for the Bucs from 1927–1940.

- **San Francisco Giants** pitcher **Matt Cain** threw a perfect game against the **Houston Astros** on June 13, 2012.

- **Montreal Expos** all-star pitcher **Dennis Martínez**, "El Presidente," threw a perfect game against the **Los Angeles Dodgers** on July 28, 1991.

- **St. Louis Cardinals** slugger **Mark Whiten** blasted four home runs in a single game against the **Cincinnati Reds** on September 7, 1993, and also drove in 12 runs—an MLB record for a lone contest.

- The famous baseball poem **"Casey at the Bat"** was written by Ernest Lawrence Thayer and first published in 1888.

- The **National Baseball Hall of Fame and Museum**, where all the legends of the game reside, is located in Cooperstown, New York.

Baseball Resources

BOOKS

Truth be told, while I have read many books relating to baseball, I didn't really use any for this work. Material like that is meant for enjoyment, not necessarily inspiration. They're just fun to read. However, as there are excellent books out there on the subject, I've recommended a few here. Check them out if you like. Your local library might carry them (hope they do):

Jim Bouton, *Ball Four* (World Publishing Company, 1970)

W. P. Kinsella, *Shoeless Joe* (Houghton Mifflin 1982)

Bernard Malamud, *The Natural* (Harcourt Brace and Company, 1952) David Neft and associates, *The Baseball Encyclopedia* (Macmillan, 1969–1996)

Geoffrey C. Ward, Ken Burns, and Kevin Baker, *Baseball: An Illustrated History* (Knopf, updated edition 2010)

WEBSITES

These sites were invaluable to my research and are truly the finest on the Web. I would recommend them highly if you enjoy baseball or if you ever need to double-check your facts:

Baseball Almanac (https://baseball-almanac.com). What a glorious site for baseball! So much information and wonderful stories on the history of the game. Highly recommended if you love the sport.

Baseball Reference (https://baseball-reference.com). The greatest gathering of baseball statistics that I have ever seen. The absolute best of the best. Without this site, I could not have written this book. To those who run it, I tip my cap!

Acknowledgments

No book is ever written alone, so I would like to express my sincere gratitude to my editor Katie McGuire, who has been kind and understanding through and through; and also to Lori Burke, who gave me the chance to write this book.
Thank you—you are the best.

About the Author

The author of a book really isn't that important. That is not false modesty. It's the words and the story that counts—or, in this particular case, the statistics! I was able to create this work solely due to the famed accomplishments of so many other talented individuals. They are the story, without a doubt. The ballplayers made this happen, so please don't forget that.

However, as I suppose I have to, I'll tell you a little bit about myself. I'm an author and poet from New England and enjoy creating trivia on various subjects. I have even written for a few newspapers in the past, with articles concerning nature and bird watching.

It was a great deal of fun writing this book and I only hope I get a chance to repeat the process. If so, perhaps I'll meet you again in another work concerning baseball. If that's the case, thank you so much for the second at-bat!

Not certain if you were able to guess by reading the book, but I am a New York Yankees fan. Which, living in New England, can sometimes make things a bit difficult with your neighbors, although it's all in good fun! However, I love baseball in all its forms, whether it be the majors or minors or even Little League. It's the game of games and means a great deal to me. It's the first sport I ever saw as a child. Whether you play it or watch it or read about it, baseball seems to have a life of its own. It's nice to be a part of it, even at a distance. I'm just a fan, like so many others. . .

In closing, I wanted to express my thanks to you, the reader, and hope you enjoyed this book. It was great to journey through the history of baseball with you by way of stats, stories, and lore. Never forget to take time out of life to stop and watch a ballgame now and then, as it'll help you stay young at heart. It's your time at the plate, so please take care of yourself—and remember, *always* keep your eye on the ball!

© 2025 by Quarto Publishing Group USA Inc.

First published in 2025 by Epic Ink,
an imprint of The Quarto Group,
142 West 36th Street, 4th Floor,
New York, NY 10018, USA
(212) 779-4972 • www.Quarto.com

Epic Ink titles are also available at discount for retail,
wholesale, promotional, and bulk purchase. For details,
contact the Special Sales Manager by email at specialsales@
quarto.com or by mail at The Quarto Group, Attn: Special
Sales Manager, 100 Cummings Center Suite 265D, Beverly,
MA 01915 USA.

10 9 8 7 6 5 4 3 2 1

ISBN: 978-0-7603-9371-0

Digital edition published in 2025
eISBN: 978-0-7603-9372-7

Library of Congress Cataloging-in-Publication Data

Names: Spada, Vincent M. (Vincent Matthew), 1976- author.
Title: The baseball ultimate trivia book : test your superfan
    status and relive the most iconic baseball moments /
    Vincent Spada.
Description: New York, NY, USA : Epic Ink, an imprint of The
    Quarto Group, 2025. | Summary: "With over 600 questions,
    facts, and quizzes from baseball history, The Baseball
    Ultimate Trivia Book gives baseball fans the chance to
    test themselves and others on baseball's most iconic
    moments"-- Provided by publisher.
Identifiers: LCCN 2024039408 (print) | LCCN 2024039409
    (ebook) | ISBN 9780760393710 (paperback)
    | ISBN 9780760393727 (ebook)
Subjects: LCSH: Baseball--Miscellanea. | Baseball
    players--Miscellanea.
Classification: LCC GV867 .S696 2025 (print) | LCC GV867
    (ebook) | DDC 796.357--dc23/eng/20240911
LC record available at https://lccn.loc.gov/2024039408
LC ebook record available at https:
    //lccn.loc.gov/2024039409

Group Publisher: Rage Kindelsperger
Creative Director: Laura Drew
Managing Editor: Cara Donaldson
Editor: Katie McGuire
Cover and Interior Design: Maeve Bargman
Illustrator: Mat Edwards

Printed in China

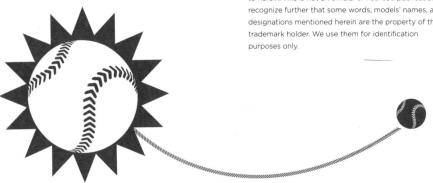